How to Thrive
in College

How to Thrive in College

Melvina Noel, Ed.D.

Outskirts Press, Inc.
Denver, Colorado

The opinions expressed in this manuscript are solely the opinions of the author and do not represent the opinions or thoughts of the publisher. The author has represented and warranted full ownership and/or legal right to publish all the materials in this book.

How to Thrive in College
All Rights Reserved.
Copyright © 2011 Melvina Noel, Ed.D.
v2.0

This book may not be reproduced, transmitted, or stored in whole or in part by any means, including graphic, electronic, or mechanical without the express written consent of the publisher except in the case of brief quotations embodied in critical articles and reviews.

Outskirts Press, Inc.
http://www.outskirtspress.com

ISBN: 978-1-4327-6869-0

Outskirts Press and the "OP" logo are trademarks belonging to Outskirts Press, Inc.

PRINTED IN THE UNITED STATES OF AMERICA

Table of Contents

Chapter One: Must Read Introduction 1
(With 5 degrees ranging from an associate to a doctorate—yes, I do know the way to earning degrees healthily and happily.)

Chapter Two: Just Breathe 9
(You already own the first key to your success. Learn how to use your breath properly to insure balance and peace of mind.)

Chapter Three: Get a New Attitude 17
(Take charge of you. Learn the way to control your brain and the way to truly love yourself.)

Chapter Four: Bring Others on Board 29
(Be patient with family, friends, employers and others but do not let them pull you away from your task at hand.)

Chapter Five: Knowledge is the Key 39
(Take time to know your college—the campus, the offices, the extra-curricular activities, and the people.)

Chapter Six: Prepare for Your First Day 47
(Be more than prepared with your materials, some advance studying, and self-care.)

Chapter Seven: The Race is On 55
(There are some must do's on the first day and the first couple of weeks. Follow them with dedication and enthusiasm. On your mark, get set, go!)

Chapter Eight: Stay Organized 63
(You are responsible for keeping your college life and your personal life running smoothly. Stay ahead of the game with these great organization tips.)

Chapter Nine: Reach for the Moon 73
(It's time to set realistic short term and long term goals. Here's a novel idea: Create a five year plan.)

Chapter Ten: A Potpourri of Do's and Don'ts 81
(Believe it or not, there are still a few more tips to make your college life more than doable. Enjoy.)

1
Must Read Introduction

All too often students open their textbooks, skip past the introduction, and head straight for Chapter One. I wanted to make sure that you did not skip the introduction this time so I am calling the introduction, Chapter One. (Pretty clever, right?) However, I am hoping that this Chapter One/Introduction will influence you to read all introductions in the future. Do you know why it is important to read the introduction? It is because the introduction provides valuable information about the format and the objectives of the book.

Now, before I provide the format and the objectives of this book, I need to make a few points. The first point is that studies show that students get more from their textbooks if they actively read. In fact, the well-known reading system called SQ3R (Survey, Question, Read, Recite, Review) which was developed by Francis Robinson, a writer and a teacher, encourages incorporating physical action into your reading. By physical action, I do not mean that you should jump up and down but if jumping up and down helps you to read; then please, be my guest!

Briefly, SQ3R is about the following: The "S" stands for "surveying" the chapter before you actually read it. It means getting an overview, focusing on the most essential points, and dividing the chapter into manageable parts. The "Q" stands for "question" and requires that you turn headings into questions before you read so that you can focus on finding the answers. The first "R" is about "reading actively" by highlighting key points and trying to predict what the author will say next. The second "R" stands for "recite" and includes orally or mentally answering questions about each section of a chapter. The third "R" is about "reviewing" the entire chapter to see what you can recall from each section.

Active reading is a crucial step in reading any chapter. Since you own your textbooks, you can use your highlighter to carefully mark key information for future study. Now, if you end up highlighting the whole page, you are having trouble distinguishing what is the most important information. Important information includes information that you might see on a quiz or test later. It includes key concepts, related vocabulary, and relevant supporting details. Of course, important information is also the information that your professor cites in the class lecture. Sometimes important information is already in bold or italicized so you do not need to highlight it but you do need to learn it. The more you practice minimizing what you highlight, the better you will become in choosing what information should be highlighted.

Besides highlighting you can write notes in the margins of your textbook. (If you prefer, you can also use a separate sheet of paper.) You can also take advantage of the margins by writing specific text-related questions. Pretend you are the professor. What information would you expect your students to know? Write the questions in the margins near the answers in the text. Then when you are studying for the test, cover up the text, read the questions, and see if you can answer them. Then check your answers in the related text. Even if you get someone to ask you the questions orally, they will be able to find the answers in the text. This technique is a great exercise for studying.

Are you starting to see the benefits of active reading? Why not give it the old college try, and make highlighting and writing margin notes two of your habits. (Of course, if you are already highlighting and writing margin notes; hurray for you!) But if you are one of those students who refuse to mark in your books because you are saving them to sell, then by all means, get some paper for your note-taking or dare to copy the entire book as I once had a student do. Go figure! I have never understood the concept of saving a textbook for resale to the point of not writing in it. You do not try to save your clothes, your car, or your house for resale. In fact, you try to get the most out of your investments by enjoying and using them to the fullest extent possible. So I, for one, can never understand saving an instrument of knowledge for resale. I, personally, want to maximize my learning by actively reading my textbooks so that the knowledge on the page becomes the knowledge in my head.

With regard to highlighting, I hope that you have found some information in this Chapter One/Introduction worth highlighting. Did you highlight the important points about the SQ3R system? Good for you! Are you curious enough to go to the Internet to search for more information pertaining to the SQ3R system or active reading in general? Bravo! An excellent student always wants to know more and acts on it by going the extra mile.

The second point that I want to make is that this Chapter One/Introduction is your first step to realizing the way to get through college stress-free. Before you start on any journey you need to get the lay of the land and you need to be reassured that you are capable of finishing your journey? You need to know that there are others who have walked the path before you who are excited about preventing you from making the same mistakes that they made. (Can you imagine how much easier our lives would have been if we had listened to our parents?) As a college student, you really can learn from mistakes that others have made and, of course, make brand new mistakes of your own. Oh yes, I can practically guarantee that you will make mistakes, but I promise you that none of your mistakes will be life threatening. However, if you are a medical student . . .

Personally, I am in love with learning as my five degrees in various subjects will support. And yes, I earned four of them while working full-time or part-time with all the same responsibilities and mishaps that affect college students today. In fact, while I was working on my doctorate and teaching part-time at a community college, I also accepted the position of being the Director of the Virginia Student Recruitment and Retention Program (VSRRP). It was tough but I needed the extra income and guess what? I still graduated with all A's in my doctoral program. (Do we have to count that A- in Statistics?) I also created brand new activities for the VSRRP, and I did not neglect my classes as my student evaluations will show. I am not suggesting that you do a thousand and one things while attending college, but I am suggesting that you do not let your desire to go to college be deterred by anyone or anything.

College is manageable is my third point. I believe with all my heart that you can manage your college life in a healthy and positive manner. There are no real barriers; only imagined ones. It does not matter whether you work full-time or part-time; whether you are married or single; whether you have children or not; or whether you graduated from high school yesterday or many moons ago. You can integrate college life into your so-called regular life without detriment to you, your family, friends, or employer. College is very doable. Let me write that again. College is very doable!

There is an article that I always share with my students during the first week of class. It's entitled, "Earning 64 Credits in a Single Semester" (The Chronicle of Higher Education, March 27, 1998, A47). To make a long story short, Eric Coyle, while a senior at the University of Nevada in Las Vegas, was taking 16 classes (2 of them at a community college) and 3 off-campus internships in one semester. In the previous semester, he completed 44 credit hours and kept up a 3.9 average. So what is my point? It is not that you should compete with Eric Coyle. In fact, I suggest that during your college stay, you should compete only with yourself by trying to do better and better. I mention Eric Coyle to show you that if he could keep an "A" average while taking 44 credit hours; there is no telling what you can achieve with the typical course load.

Your steadfastness and ability to lighten-up are the determining factors for experiencing college with minimum stress. Once you make the commitment to physically, mentally, and spiritually invest in going to college; that is, once you commit with every fiber of your being; everything will fall into place to support you. It is when you are truly committed enough to move forward without reservation that nobody or nothing can take you off the college path. And if you are committed, this book will provide the tools for helping you to add peace of mind to your commitment. And yes, I do mean "peace" and not "piece."

Going to college can be one of the easiest undertakings of your life. Do you know why? Because the minimum requirement is that you show up and take an active role in your learning. (Remember, this book is not about the procedures that are required to get into a particular college. If you are at that stage, you are looking for another book. Check with your librarian, the Internet, and other sources for information on finding the right college for you, application procedures, financial aid, etc.) Keep this book on hand to show you how to maximize your enjoyment of college.

Before I provide the format and the objectives of this book, I want to elaborate on the need for you to have a "love for learning." Have you ever been in love? Of course, you have. Do you remember how you felt? For me, everything was covered in giggles. The grass seemed greener and the sky bluer. Oh, the power of love!

You need to fall madly in love with wanting to learn in every class irregardless of whether the subject is in your major field of study or not, and irregardless of whether you like your professor or not. Know that you are capable of learning any subject put before you. In fact, you are more than capable! Your capability will never be an issue. More likely than not, the issue will be about how much of yourself are you willing to invest in your studies.

Look at it this way! What happens when you purchase an item as small as an ink pen and you find out it doesn't write? You want it exchanged right away. What if the purchase is as big as a house and you find a problem with the plumbing? You want it fixed right away. What happens after you find the college you want, get accepted, go through the tedious registration procedures, and pay all your expenses? You want to get out of class early, to do minimum class work, and to have little or no homework. In other words, college is the only place where you want less for your money instead of more.

After teaching for over twenty years, I have not yet had a class to take me up on my offer of staying a half hour or longer beyond class time. When I am in the zone (the teaching zone), I sometimes say to my students, "I'm excited. Why don't we stay longer? It won't cost you anything. Actually, you will be getting more for your money." My students either laugh or look at me like I'm crazy. Would their reaction be different if I were offering a clothing sale where they could buy one item and get one item free? But I digress.

Know that no one can ever take your earned degree away from you. They can take your car, your home, and other material goods but your degree and the knowledge you have gained is yours forever to do with as you please. It is a sure investment. So why not enjoy the journey of minimizing stress and maximizing enjoyment in college? Let us begin this journey with the format of the chapters in this book. Each chapter will fully discuss the subject at hand with humorous anecdotes, references to valuable resources, and practical learning activities. The goals of this book are as follows:

(1) To keep you turning the pages so that you will get the full benefit of all the information between these covers.

(2) To encourage you to never give up; that is, once you have entered college you have nowhere else to go but to finish.

(3) To provide you with specific practical tools to integrate your college life with your regular life.

(4) To share information and experiences that will help create a productive learning experience in a stress-free manner.

(5) To show you the way to create a well-rounded college life.

Before I bring this Chapter One/Introduction to a close, I would like you to ponder a couple of ideas. Think of your college journey as a positive journey into enlightenment, excitement, and fun. Yes, learning can be a lot of fun. If you endeavor to experience every class with enthusiasm, joy, and love; you will know what I mean. Do not expect that your professor must be entertaining. If you get an enthusiastic, entertaining professor; then thank your lucky stars. If you get a boring, monotone, put-you-to-sleep professor; then still, thank your lucky stars. What you take from the class depends on your attitude! Be greedy. Seek knowledge. It is through college that you will have actually set aside specific times by way of your classes to just gather knowledge. How fabulous is that? (Are you jumping up and down with enthusiasm yet?)

And yes, sometimes your grades may fall, your spirit may dampen, and your attitude may be negative but as with everything in life, you will pick yourself up, brush yourself off, get back on your feet, and move forward. Even when you are in love, there can be a few bumps in the road! But even then, it is through patience that you can level those bumps. Focus on the present moment so that you can create the future that you deserve. The reason why you decided to go to college in the first place was for a brighter future, right?

Enough! If I keep talking this way you will think I am mad. What sane person is this enthusiastic about college? All lovers of knowledge! Obtaining knowledge is a win-win situation. You have everything to gain. So, I implore you to learn the way to enjoying college by perusing this lovely book, one informative page at a time.

Activities

Write any questions, notes, comments, and must do's for yourself in the margins. Use your highlighter on at least three key points. As you continue reading, keep your highlighter in your hand and a pen or pencil nearby. Use them appropriately. Let's read on with love and enthusiasm!

2
Just Breathe

I suspect that after reading the title of this chapter you are wondering what, if anything, does breathing have to do with managing your college life. Plus, isn't breathing a natural process? Yes, of course it is, but most people breathe in an unnatural way. I will talk about this in a moment. For now, let me say that by practicing conscious and controlled deep breathing, you will create balance and stability within your being which will in turn have a positive impact on how you experience your college life. Does that sound like a good deal?

I need you to do a little homework or I should say "observation" work. The next time you are near an infant, study carefully how that infant is breathing. With each inhalation, the infant's abdomen expands and with each exhalation, the infant's abdomen contracts. In other words, the infant inhales the breath all the way down into the abdomen as opposed to the typical shallow breathing into the chest that we are more apt to do as we get older. It is unfortunate that too many people without realizing it disconnect from the natural and correct way of being, not only with breathing, but with regard to other aspects of their true selves. Our natural way to breathe becomes hampered by our actions and reactions to the vicissitudes of life.

The good news is that you can get back to correct breathing with knowledge and practice. Why should you invest in learning conscious and controlled deep breathing techniques now when you have survived just fine all your life with the way you have been breathing? The answer is very clear. Conscious and controlled deep breathing is a major key to stress-free living and in turn, a stress-free college life. Isn't it great how knowledge works? One subject can cross over into other areas and make a positive difference. It is important that I show you the incredible effects of conscious and controlled deep breathing before I go any further. I believe that the more knowledge you have about the benefits of conscious and controlled deep breathing; the higher the probability that you will create time in your life to practice conscious and controlled deep breathing on a daily basis. The more you practice, the more the chances are that conscious and controlled deep breathing will become your natural way of breathing.

Of course, the hardest part of any new program in life is taking that first step. So, my immediate task is to convince you to at least take the first step. After that, I am not worried because once you experience the relaxing effects of deep breathing; you will make time in your life to practice. The beauty of deep breathing is that too much does not add calories or cause an overdose—it's all good! And guess what? Those of you who are already doing breath work can still benefit from reading this chapter. I am sure of it!

Let's begin with that first breath of air that the newborn inhales into the lungs to begin this earthly life. Remember it was not too long ago when you were that baby! (Too bad I can't say the same for me.) In Barbara Larsen's book, *The Perfect Moment*, we are reminded that the breath is the most basic form of life nourishment. (I bet you thought it was milk.) Larsen emphasizes that you cannot do slow deep breathing and have a panic attack or stay extremely angry. The physical body just cannot do both at the same time. Do you get the full impact of this statement? Let me show you.

First, consider deep breathing for controlling panic attacks. How many exams do you expect you will be taking during the course of your college life? Hundreds! And some of those tests, such as mid-terms and final exams, may be worth such a large percentage of your grade that they may make the difference in whether you pass or fail the course. On top of that, many of your future employers will use your transcript as one of the sources to determine whether they hire you or not. Pressure will try to engulf you but it is with your breath that you will break the chains of pressure and learn to relax before, during, and after your test. It is with your very own breath that you will keep a clear mind so that all your focus and energy is on responding correctly to test questions.

As an aside, I sometimes teach an essay writing class where the students are required to write a 350 word essay in one hour and twenty minutes for their final exam. The pressure that they feel is tremendous because even if they have a passing average in their course work, they cannot pass the course unless they pass the final essay. So how do I help them to minimize their stress? I spend about fifteen minutes of one class period teaching them how to do conscious and controlled deep breathing. The beauty is that my students get to experience, maybe for the first time in their lives, the immediate calming effect of their own breath. Of course, I encourage them to practice deep breathing on a regular basis but whether they do or not, I don't know. What I do know is that on the day of their final exam, they do practice with sincerity and knowledge that stress is one less thing that they will have to worry about while writing their final essays.

But taking tests is only one of the many stressors in college. Students often see their professors as stressors. They insist that their professors are too boring or too talkative, too strict or too lax, too short or too tall—the list is never-ending. Before I show you how using conscious and controlled deep breathing can relieve you of stressing about your professors, I want to remind you that each of your professors will have a different personality. They are, after all, human beings. Try to always remember that no two human beings are alike. Embrace the differences in your professors and just do what you signed up for; that is, learn the lessons.

To defend professors, students oftentimes forget that professors were not hired to be entertainers but to teach the subject matter. And to defend students, you have the right to report a professor that is not fully engaged in "teaching" you. However, I suggest that you speak to that professor first. I have found that many issues are basically misunderstandings that can be resolved with a one-on-one meeting.

If you are still wondering how you can learn from a professor whom you do not like for one reason or another, let me tell you how. Use slow deep breathing to stop the useless chattering of your brain because it is really your brain that is giving you all that grief. As you focus on your breath, your brain will begin to quiet the constant chatter. As you continue deep breathing, you will be able to get back to calmness and clear thinking. Try it. The proof is in the doing. Deep breathing is like one of those money-back guarantee items. If it doesn't work, then you can go back to being stressed.

I suspect that if you have had no training in breath work, you may feel that what I have said sounds too simple and maybe even unbelievable. Barbara Larsen (*The Perfect Moment*) explains that guided breathing quiets the mind and tells the body to relax. It is with a quiet mind and a relaxed body that you will be more in tune with your studies and not focused on the personality of your professor.

Remember also that there are other college personnel—those people at the registration office who rush you through lines without listening to your side of the story; counselors who direct you in the wrong direction; administrators who always take the professor's side; or security that won't give your car battery a jump. (You see, I have experienced it all even though the aforementioned examples rarely happen!) How do you deal with so many different personalities without pulling your hair out? (Of course, if you are already bald, you have got it made.) Matthew Ignoffo in his book, *Coping with Your Inner Critic*, explains that one of the oldest and simplest forms of calming yourself is breathing deeply while listening to the sound of your breath. Ignoffo adds that in any situation breathing deeply is helpful for clearing your mind if you get tense.

Even when your college day goes smoothly, your so-called regular life might be bumpy. There will be days when your spouse or significant other is driving you mad or you want to disown your child or the day just is not going your way. How do you keep yourself balanced and happy? I know you know the answer by now. But just in case you are having a memory lapse: practice conscious and controlled deep breathing.

I want to reiterate that it is with your breath work that you will react to negative situations in a more relaxed and positive manner. Try this idea on for size. You never have to react to people in a negative way just because they are behaving badly. If you act as they do, then what is the difference between you and them? Nothing! So instead of an immediate volatile reaction, inhale slowly into your abdomen to the count of seven; hold your breath in your abdomen to the count of seven; and exhale slowly to the count of seven. Make sure all of your attention is on your breath moving slowing through your body. Inhale and exhale very slowly until calmness overtakes you. I promise you that calmness will arrive if you really focus only on your breath. Before you know it, you will be in the wonderful, magical place called the *present moment*. I say "magical" because all too often we are focused on the past or the future such that it will probably feel magical to be physically, mentally, and spiritually in the present moment. Do not be surprised if focusing on your breath causes your lips to turn upward into a smile. You might even giggle.

There is only one other major point that I need to address before I close this chapter with a deep breathing exercise especially tailored for you. Another very important benefit of breath work is that deep breathing will increase your oxygen intake. Professor Nader Angha in his book, *Expansion and Contraction within Being,* presents a comprehensive discussion on breathing with regard to the entire universe. However, I am only going to focus on the information that Professor Nader Angha provides concerning the impact of deep breathing with regard to human beings. He explains that in normal breathing 0.5 liter of air enters the lungs while with deep breathing the oxygen intake is increased by ten times as much. For those of you who do not want to do the math, that is five liters of oxygen.

So you're probably thinking, more oxygen—big deal! Yes, it is a very big deal. Without getting too technical (for my sake, not yours), oxygen intake enhances the energy production of the body which in turn results in the strengthening of the body's immune system. Professor Nader Angha explains this in great detail in his book. What is most important is that the more conscious deep breathing you do, the more you will create a healthier and more energetic body. In fact, Professor Nader Angha sees deep breathing as an important preventative factor in disease control and treatment. So practicing deep breathing will minimize your missing classes and assignments due to illness; will maximize your energy for enjoying the college experience; and will facilitate a positive integration of your college life with your regular life.

I hope that by now I have convinced you that conscious and controlled deep breathing will not only help create the right attitude for a successful college life, but it will enhance your total well-being. I hope that you will try the following deep breathing exercise for a minimum of ten minutes (working up to thirty minutes) before you go to bed at night and/or when you get up in the morning. If you are going to fight with me about how you do not have the time, know that it is even beneficial to practice conscious and controlled deep breathing for five to ten minutes at various times during the day than not to practice at all. You own your breath. Why not take advantage of its many benefits?

Activity

Find a quiet space. Sit cross-legged on the floor with your shoulders back and your spine straight. Place your hands (palms up) on your knees. Relax. Start inhaling very slowly and deeply through your nose. Make sure to push your breath down to your abdomen so that your abdomen expands. Hold your breath there for a few moments. Then exhale very slowly deflating your abdomen and following your breath back up and through your mouth. Continue breathing in this manner, making sure that you are focused on the movement and the sound of your breath.

Do not worry about the mental chatter of your brain. The chatter will start to dissipate the more you focus on your breath. You might not clear your mind in one sitting but over time you will have less and less chatter. Your only goal is to inhale and exhale long and slow while you focus on feeling and hearing your breath.

Make conscious and controlled deep breathing a habit. I invite you to take meditation or yoga classes, but whether you do or not, you need to make deep breathing a part of your daily routine. Don't you eat and sleep every day? Well, deep breathing is just as important for enhancing your mental, physical, and spiritual health.

3

Get a New Attitude

Have you heard that song by Patti Labelle called, "New Attitude"? She sings the following words with spirited energy and a finger popping beat:

I'm feeling good from my head to my shoes,
Know where I am going and I know what to do,
I've tidied up my point of view,
I've got a new attitude.

Do you know where you are going and what you need to do? You are going to college where you must keep taking class after class until you receive your degree. You will need to tidy up your point of view such that maybe for the first time in your life you will have to put your needs first. It does not mean that you will be selfish, but it does mean that you will not let anyone or anything deter you from your goal of finishing your education. It does mean that you deserve to be as loving and generous to yourself as you are to others. You see, I am absolutely sure that you are a loving and generous person. Didn't you buy two copies of this book, one for you and the other for a friend? If not, don't worry. You still have time.

Your responsibility as a student is to succeed in obtaining your degree. To quote Jesse Jackson, "If my mind can conceive it, and my heart can believe it, I know I can achieve it." Consider letting your mantra be, "I will get my degree." And don't just think about it. Take action. Write it down. Post it on the refrigerator. Post it on the mirror in the bathroom. Say it out loud on a regular basis. Keep your enthusiasm up by believing in yourself. Do not let family problems, financial issues, the vicissitudes of college life, or anything keep you from moving forward.

Actually, I think one of the main reasons why there are college drop-outs is because students have the misconception that the overall experience of college will get easier as they progress. Yes, it gets easier in that you are more familiar with different aspects of college but your professors and the subject matter will become more demanding as you take courses in your major field of study. You will find yourself needing more "quality and quantity" time for your studies even though the one thing that you will find that you have so precious little of is time.

Look at it this way. Going through your college years is quite similar to being in a long distance marathon. The first leg of a race is usually fairly easy, right? The runners are full of energy and hopeful that they will win the race. This is the same kind of energy that you will bring to your first year of college. As the race progresses, the runners experience thirst, sore muscles, tiredness, mental stress—well, you get the picture. Some of the runners are now hoping that they just finish the race, never mind winning.

Like the runners, over a period of time, the demands of college life will create sore muscles, tiredness, mental stress, and even thoughts of quitting. Let me assure you that wanting to quit every now and then is perfectly normal! It might even be healthy. Many runners want to quit halfway through the race but they keep going on just as you must keep going on.

The funny thing is that the closer you get to the finish line, the more you may want to quit, not just because of the demanding requirements and the high expectations of professors in your major field of study; but because you are truly exhausted. You start wondering if it is all worth it. You even question why you came to college in the first place. Your mind reminds you that there are successful people who never went to college. You could be one of them. Right?

Wrong! You know in your heart that college is the direction that you need to go to create the kind of life that you personally want. That's why you started in the first place. Remember? Do not let your brain sidetrack you. Whatever it takes, you must finish. Nothing in life is a piece of cake except of course, a piece of cake. It is your responsibility to keep a positive attitude until you cross the finish line. Aren't you always excited for those runners who cross the finish line? Some of them cross it and fall flat to the ground. (Don't worry. They do get up, brush themselves off, and get on with their lives.) You have to do the same thing. You have to keep going on until you cross the finish line.

Sure, there will be times when you want to cut class, scream at a professor, or just rip up a test. Trust me, after earning five degrees I can pretty much guarantee that I have experienced all the negative emotions that crop up while attending college. It is because I was banged up quite a bit, metaphorically speaking, of course, during my college years that I can now show you how to protect yourself from the stressful situations that exist on practically every college campus. The very best way to create a stress-free environment is to get "a new attitude" by (1) controlling your thoughts and (2) loving yourself.

Controlling Your Thoughts

Your brain can sometimes be your worst enemy. How many times have you left your house and several miles down the road, your brain asks you, "Did you leave the stove on?" Now, why didn't you get that question before you left the house? Or how is it that when something bad happens to you, instead of just forgetting about it and getting on with your life, your brain plays the scene over and over again like a bad song that you cannot get out of your head. In fact, for a great majority of people, their brain is in constant chatter; mostly negative and worrisome chatter about what's already happened in the past or what might happen in the future. In Professor Sadegh Angha's book, *The Mystery of Humanity: Tranquility and Survival,* he suggests that thoughts that do not give inner peace and tranquility are useless and knowledge that does not enhance the personality is worthless. Ponder that for a moment!

So how do you control the "negative" mental chatter and replace it with a blank slate so that you can experience inner peace and tranquility? First, you need to be fully aware of how busy your mind stays. Try this little experiment. Set your clock to alarm in three minutes. Have paper and pen on hand. Close your eyes. (Okay, you need to finish reading this paragraph first.) Let your mind do its thing. In other words, do not try to control your thoughts. Just be aware of them and see where they take you. Now, you can close your eyes and keep them closed until your alarm rings.

Three minutes up? Okay. Write. Where did your thoughts take you? Were the majority of your thoughts negative or positive? Did you have any moments when you did not think about anything? Okay, do it again. Set the clock to alarm in three minutes but this time when you close your eyes, do your best to control your thoughts. Okay, go!

Were you able to control your thoughts? I would not be surprised if your brain rambled just as much or even more when you tried to control it. The good news is that everyone has the potential to be the master of his or her mind. Of course, I have already made you aware of one of the most important ways to minimize chatter; that is, by practicing conscious and controlled deep breathing as discussed in Chapter Two. I hope that you have decided to make deep breathing as much a part of your life as eating regular meals. Actually, you may benefit by missing a couple of meals but you will never benefit by missing a couple of deep breathing sessions! Conscious and controlled deep breathing is one of those subjects that require minimum discussion and maximum action. The command, "just do it!" comes to mind.

Another way to rid your mind of negative thoughts is to replace them with positive thoughts. When my mind is running amuck, I rein it in quickly with a special prayer that I repeat. I do mean, "Repeat." I say my special prayer from the beginning to the end repeatedly until I no longer remember what thoughts were bothering me. Actually, more times than not, my mind is free before I finish my prayer the first time around, but I like to repeat it to insure that I have worked off all possibility of my negative thoughts returning. Whether you choose to repeat a prayer or a positive mantra, what you are doing is giving your brain healthy thoughts to feed on instead of negative thoughts. Your mantra with regard to college could be something like, "I am an excellent college student who loves going to college." Your brain will begin to agree with you and you will start to act accordingly.

You can always control your thoughts by focusing on the *present*, *now*, and *this very moment*. Where are you right now? What are you doing right now? Are you reading this passage or are you thinking about something else? If you are thinking about something else, shouldn't you be doing that instead of reading this passage? Wherever you are physically, that is where you should be mentally. You cannot function properly in two different places at the same time. When you are not in the present moment, you tend to make mistakes and create problems for yourself.

Have you ever considered how many problems are caused by people not being in the present moment? Have you ever locked your keys in your car? What was the reason? Was it because you were not functioning in the present moment? Were you thinking or worrying about something in the past even though you have no control over the past? Or were you thinking or worrying about the future even though, again, you literally have no control over the future? The funny thing is the only real time that you do have control over is the present time. However, it is the present moment that eludes most people even though the reality is that no one can ever get the present moment back.

What must you do to stay in the present moment? In her book, *The Art of Sufi Healing,* Linda O'Riordan suggests that we must stop recycling the past and start evolving by consciously choosing what we think about and what we say to ourselves in order to create a better future. So it really can be as simple as choosing to be in the present. Being in the present requires working on yourself whether it is through taking a meditation or yoga class; studying and learning techniques to control your thoughts; or being aware of your thoughts so that you can erase or replace them. The bottom line is that you have to take an active role in keeping your thoughts in the present moment.

Loving Yourself

Besides working on controlling your thoughts, the other major attitude adjustment requires learning to truly love you. John Bradshaw, the author of *Healing the Shame that Binds You,* explains that self-love is recognizing that there has never been anyone like you nor will there ever be anyone like you again. He adds that each person is unique, unrepeatable, and precious. What is the proof of your uniqueness? Take a look at your fingers. In the entire universe there is no one else who has your fingerprints.

Now, go look in the mirror. (Don't forget to take this book with you.) Smile. You are a divine being who is the highest of the Creator's creations. For those of you who always wished to be an angel, let me remind you that the Creator created you superior to the angel. Prove me right by doing some research. Have I convinced you of how special you are yet? Just one more point. Not only was the human being created superior to the angel, but the holy books state that the Creator breathed His spirit into the human being. I do not think it gets better than that and maybe that is why being aware of your breath is so important.

So how does one actively invest in self-love? I am sure you can think of one hundred and one ways to be good to yourself that range from buying an expensive box of chocolates to taking a well-deserved world cruise. If buying things and going places make you happy and you can afford it, help yourself. However, there are three ingredients, if you will, that will help you to better love and nourish who you are as a human being, which in turn, will translate into you being a better and more productive student.

Before I give you the three ingredients, you need to be aware of the fact that if you are not committed to loving yourself, you will be pulled in many directions like a puppet attached to many strings; like a leaf blowing in a strong and powerful wind; like a—well, you get the picture. Students who are committed to loving themselves will have the patience and perseverance necessary for a pleasant college experience. Students committed to loving themselves will be steadfast, positive, and of course, stress-free. So, what are the three key ingredients to loving yourself that will have a positive impact on your college life? You need to (1) be grateful, (2) let go, and (3) be true to you.

Be grateful. Being grateful at first glance might seem unrelated to a stress-free college life but being grateful for everyone and everything in your life—the good, the bad, the ups, the downs—will help you to stay in balance. When you are in balance you do not react to every little thing. When you are in balance you are careful to choose your battles. Being truly grateful, not just saying the words, but being grateful from the core of your being changes the colors of your world from dark shadows and grays to sunny yellows and brilliant reds. (Okay, if you haven't guessed already; I'm also a poet.) Let me show you how being grateful works.

Let's say you get a professor who is strict beyond the meaning of the word. She is one of those professors who locks the door at the exact time the class starts to insure there are no latecomers. Now, you have always been on time, even fifteen or more minutes early, but on this particular day you are late. Your professor can actually see you coming down the hall but she still closes and locks the door. You know that you will not be able to get in until break time, an hour or so after class starts. You know this rule because it is actually written in bold letters in the syllabus and others who have been late have been locked out. Before now, you have not had a problem with this rule. What should you do? Would banging on the door and screaming help? I doubt it. It would probably only make matters worse.

As an alternative, I suggest that you inhale deeply and be very grateful. (I can hear you shouting, "Grateful for what?") Be grateful that this is the first time you have been late and you know how to make sure that you are never late again. Be grateful that your ears are sensitive enough for you to sit outside the classroom door and still hear the lecture. Be grateful that you have your books and can follow along. Be grateful that your professor has regular office hours so you can make an appointment to see her and discuss what you missed. Be grateful that you have three of your classmates' phone numbers and/or e-mail addresses so that you can get notes from one of them later. (You did exchange contact information with at least three other students in the first week of class, didn't you?)

And what will all this gratefulness do for you? As you will come to see, if you follow through with gratefulness, you will minimize stress and negative reactions. When you work on being grateful all the time regardless of the "good" or "bad" of the situation, you start leaning toward always being in balance because you will start to see the "up" side of every situation. Gordon MacDonald in his book, *A Resilient Life,* has written an entire chapter entitled, "Resilient People Overflow with Gratitude." One very important point that he makes in this chapter is that gratefulness is a learned transaction.

How do you learn to be grateful? Practice. Practice!! Practice!!! I suggest that before reacting to any situation, you breathe deeply while you focus on the positives. Then begin out loud saying, "I am grateful" and name at least three reasons. If you really cannot see any positives in your situation, then let me give you a couple. Say, "I am grateful to be pursuing my college education." Say, "I am grateful to be alive." Say, "I am grateful for this book." (Okay, I couldn't resist the third reason.) When you are grateful, you become more gentle and caring within your being, and you maintain a peace of mind.

Let go. Letting go is about getting rid of any preconceived ideas about what you expect your college experience to be like. As human beings we tend to create stories for ourselves for every new situation. I can promise you that what you envision will never match the reality. For example, my students often tell me that they never expected so much homework. The truth is homework is usually assigned from the first day of class to the last. Why? New information seems clear when you are in front of the professor; however, it is when you are on your own at home that new information may become confusing or downright unintelligible.

Students also have preconceived ideas of what should be taught and how it should be taught. They bring with them the baggage of what they learned in the past and use that for the foundation of new information. That does not always work. Actually, the easiest way to learn a new subject is by letting go of some of your past learning. The best way I can explain it to you is by example. As I write this book, I am also teaching an essay writing class to non-native speakers. Oftentimes, what I teach them about the format of the essay does not match what they learned in previous classes so there are always a couple of students who begin their comments or questions with, "Well, I learned in my other class . . ." and I generously always give them their three minutes of fame before I try to bring them into the light.

I begin by assuring them that what they learned is correct but there are different kinds of writing. In my class, they will be learning formal essay writing with a few different twists and turns than what they learned in other writing classes. Then their immediate concern becomes what to do with what they have already learned. I say, "Let go!" and their mouths drop. Some students even get angry with me. I explain that they will not lose what they learn but they need to put it on the back burner for now. I look out across the class to see some mouths still open and to see some lips turned upside down into frowns.

"Okay, look at it this way," I say, as I walk to the blackboard. I draw a picture of two glasses, one full almost to the rim with water and the other with less than a quarter glass of water. I label the full glass "A" and the other glass "B." Then I ask the million dollar question. If I want to add water, which glass can I get the most water in? Of course, the answer is obvious and yet, it is so difficult to understand that one must do the same for learning. In order to truly learn, one must be empty, if you will, to allow new information to find its rightful place in the brain. It is difficult to learn new information when you keep comparing the new to the old. Once you learn the new information, you may be able to integrate the old with the new or you may find that the old information is no longer useful for the new subject at hand.

The bottom line is that college is not a place to be set in your ways. It is about knowledge, remember? Learning requires openness and the ability to change. Openness enhances a state of balance and peace of mind. The ability to change prevents rigidity and tension. Stress comes when you think knowledge is set in stone. Come on; look at the advancements in technology. Letting go can translate into mental freedom and a productive learning experience.

You be you. The world renowned Sufi Master, Professor Nader Angha, says on a regular basis in his lectures, "You be you." On first glance, it appears to be a very simple sentence but it is packed with meaning and power on many different levels. When you act according to the meaning of "you be you"; you will begin to present yourself as you were created to be. Instead of being jerked around by people and life's circumstances, you will live from inside-out instead of from outside-in. You will exist as a human "being" as opposed to always rushing through life as a human "doing."

Being true to yourself has to do with making decisions in your life that reflect who you are and not what others want you to be. Unfortunately, in most cases, people want for you what they want for themselves. In other words, it really has nothing to do with you. I think one of the most misused phrases is "If I were you, I would . . ." First of all, you are not me so any advice you give me will be about you. Maybe the phrase should begin, "From what I know about you, you might want to consider . . ." and then give the advice. However, no matter the phrasing, it is still rare for anybody to know who you really are so regardless of the advice, at the end of the day you have to be true to yourself.

Of course, it does not cost you anything to listen to advice from every Tom, Dick, and Jane. But it will cost you everything, if you take advice that is not true to you. I am talking about the "you" who has made a commitment to go to college and to get the most out of it. I am talking about the "you" who should not be bullied into majoring in a field you do not like because others expect you to do so. I am talking about the "you" who should not feel obligated to join or invest in extra-curricular activities unless they work for you. In the end, you have to remember that this is your college experience. "You be you."

Activities

Be grateful. *Take time to create a beautiful sign that asks, "What are you grateful for?" Place the sign on the refrigerator or any place where you are guaranteed to see it every day. At least once before the day is over, make sure that you have responded to the question.*

Letting go. *Check in with yourself when you feel you must have your way on an issue. Ask yourself if things must be the way you want them or is this a time when you should just "let go"?*

You be you. *Who are you? Take a few moments and respond to the following statements as quickly as possible without pondering. Once you have finished, analyze your answers. Why did you give a particular answer? Do you want to change any answers and if so, why?*

If I were a piece of fruit, I would be _____.
If I were a color, I would be _____.
If I were a flower, I would be _____.

If I were an article of clothing, I would be _____.
If I were an instrument, I would be _____.
If I were a moment in time, I would be _____.
If I were a/an _____, I would be _____.

4
Bring Others on Board

You have to integrate your college life into your personal life in a positive manner. In other words you have to maintain balance between your new college life, family, friends, employers, and others. When you create such a balance you will come closer to functioning as a stress-free productive student. The key is to make an effort to bring everybody on board such that they are on your team instead of working against you. Easier said than done? Sometimes. Sometimes not.

Family. Let's look at your family first. Your family's support of you attending college will fit into one of three categories: (1) they will provide great support and inspiration; (2) they will fight you tooth and nail; or (3) they will be apathetic. Category one is the best category because a supportive family automatically puts you in a win-win situation. Jump up and down and thank your lucky stars if your family is supportive. Great support means your family not only talks the talk but they walk the walk. Specifically, they will put forth the time and energy to help make your college life easier. All you will have to do is let them know what they need to do to support you. No, I don't mean they should become your slaves. What I do mean is that you should have a tentative plan for sharing responsibilities that includes everything from cooking, cleaning, running errands and allowing you quiet, study time. Once you have presented your tentative plan, allow family members to add their suggestions so that you can create the formal plan together. This formal plan, of course, is still not written in stone and should be adjusted as needed.

Now if your family is from category 2; that is, they fight you tooth and nail; they can cause you the greatest harm if you are not strong. Their goal will be to hold on to the way things have always been and to make you feel guilty for seeking change. Unfortunately, it is about their wants and needs. They need for you to continue to be the spouse, parent, sibling, or friend that you have always been and any change like going to college is a threat to that.

You might think it is selfish of your family not to enthusiastically support you for wanting to go to college. Well, you are right. It is selfish of them but try to understand their point of view. In their minds, if you go to college you will take something away from the relationship that they already have with you. Of course, to a certain extent they are right but the bottom line is that you deserve to do something just for you. And most importantly, when you finish your education you will have more to offer your family.

If you are a parent going to college, let me remind you that it is not a good thing that too often moms and dads take better care of their families than they do themselves. Let me say that again more emphatically. *It is not a good thing to take better care of your family than you take care of yourself!* You must first take care of you. The result will be that you will then have more love and energy to take care of your family. How well can you take care of them when you are unhappy with your life? No matter how many people you have to support or answer to, no matter the magnitude of responsibilities in your daily life, and no matter this or that, you must always take time to do something special for yourself. The quality of your life and your family members will depend on how well you take care of you; and the only time to take care of you is now. You will not have time to do it after you die.

Of course, going to college cannot be compared to going to a spa or going on a vacation, but it is to some extent your self-care time; that is, it is the time you have set aside to take care of your needs. In other words, going to college is your vacation from the status quo to the type of future you want. This is what you must make clear to your family. You literally need to have a formal meeting around the kitchen table, if you will, to discuss this journey you are about to undertake. Before you have that meeting, make sure that you are clear about what you want to say. It is a good idea to prepare answers for what you suspect will be the opposing arguments. Your future college life is on trial here, and you need to be a good defense attorney. Remember that no matter what your family's arguments, you will not be deterred from your stance of going to college. You are definitely going but your goal is to try to bring your family on board so that you can have the type of positive support that will enhance your college life.

What's the best way to attack this meeting? (Did I say *attack?*) See, a little slip like that can cause all kinds of problems. The better question is what is the best way to conduct this meeting? First, ask your family members to just listen while you say everything you have to say before they add their two cents worth. (Did I say *two cents?*) If you allow them to interrupt you as you speak, you run the risk of never saying everything that you planned to say. Keep the meeting pleasant and uplifting because the truth of the matter is that going to college is a good thing. There are no negatives to getting an education.

You should begin the meeting with a list of reasons why going to college is important to you. The prepared list will also help you to be fully aware of your reasons for going to college and it will insure that you keep steadfast on the path to finishing. Second, let them know with passionate, loving words (1) how much you care for all of them, (2) how things are going to change but in a good way, and (3) how you really want their support in this endeavor. Take time to fully support the aforementioned three points. Emphasize how going to college will make you a happier and healthier person. When you are investing in what pleases you, there will be more sunshine in your life and that light will not only benefit you, but it will shine on and benefit others. When you have fully explained yourself, end with your bottom line. What's your bottom line? It is that you are going to go to college no matter what. That is never up for discussion.

If your family members do not interrupt you, you will get the secure feeling that they are mentally cheering you on. *Not!* Well, you might be one of the lucky ones who put forth such a good argument that the family members now fit into category one: supportive and inspirational. However, I suggest you brace yourself for what is more likely to happen. *Who's going to cook dinner? Who's going to help us with our homework? You are the parent; you're not supposed to go to school! Don't you love us anymore?* I could go on and on but what would be the point? Entertainment? Yes. The reality is that you have a responsibility to respond to your family's questions with honesty, love, and workable solutions. For example, now that you are going to college, it is as good a time as any for everybody to take turns preparing dinner. Plus, you should always keep frozen dinners, individual salads, boiled eggs, luncheon meats, fruits, and nuts on hand for quick meals and snacks. You are already doing that? Good for you. Now that you have mealtime under control, how about getting your entire household more organized? You might want to read and follow some of the helpful suggestions in "Part V: The Home" and "Part VI: Family and Lifestyle" in *Getting Organized* by Stephanie Winston.

Think of this time as time for you to do something for you, not to the neglect of your family, but with the help of your family. Their help is the love and support that you need as opposed to the "I love you" because you cook, clean, and practically work yourself to death. Do you get the big picture?

What about the apathetic family in category three? Of course, apathy is not a form of support but on the positive side, if your family members are apathetic at least they will not be giving you any grief. If you are the kind of person who needs familial support, look to family members outside of your immediate family. Uncles, aunts, cousins or distant relatives may provide the support that you need.

Friends. Is there really such a thing as peer pressure? Absolutely! It doesn't matter whether you are nine or ninety; we all want our friends to support our endeavors. When we call them up and announce that we are going to college, we are hoping for a "Wonderful. Good for you! Let's go out and celebrate." You certainly are not expecting to hear words like "Maybe you're too old to go to college" or "Your first responsibility is to your family" or "What's going to happen to our friendship—our luncheons, our shopping times, our phone conversations?" If your friends do respond negatively, then you must use the same tact that you did with your family. Remind your friends that you are not leaving the country so your special times will not be eliminated. At worst, your special times will be minimized.

Now, I must warn you. Be prepared to lose some of your so-called friends along the way but know that your true friends will be there to support you and your family in any way that you need them. I remember when I was working on my doctorate I lost many of my so-called friends because I no longer had time for a robust social life. (Well, my social life was never really "robust" anyway.) My true friends helped me with my household chores and my errands. One special friend even brought me a microwave with the insistence that I needed a faster way to warm up my meals. (Yes, I was still warming up my meals on the stove). My heart is still warmed (pun intended) by such a thoughtful gift.

It is a wonderful bonus to have the support of your friends but if you do not, you always, and I mean always, can depend on yourself. You are the very best friend that you could ever have for the rest of your life. You must never forget that!

Your Employer. So should you tell your employer that you are going to go to college? Yes, you should. No, you should not. Maybe. No, I am not trying to confuse you. There are several variables that you must consider such as the type of job you have, your relationship or non-relationship with your employer, and the conflict or non-conflict of your work hours with your class hours.

If your employer will pay for your education and you want to take advantage of that, then—no brainer—you must tell your employer. If your employer does not pay for your education and there is no conflict with the hours you go to work and the hours you plan to take your classes, it is not necessary to tell your employer. Sure, you can if you want, but before you do, make a list of the pros and cons of telling your employer because I am sorry to say that some employers, for reasons of their own, see college as a competitor. What they see is an employee who will be dividing his or her time between work and college; and most importantly, they see an employee who may soon leave the job.

Now the truth of the matter is that for most of us, our jobs are first and college is second. (If you are living at home with mom and dad, and they are footing your college bill, then maybe you can put college first and your job second.) But for the great majority of college students, no job means they lose shelter, food, and the money to pay for college. So these college students must always make sure that there is no conflict between college and their jobs. Sometimes this is very difficult because many jobs have hours that are not as clear cut as a straight eight hour shift. Some nine to five jobs spill into other hours of the day, some jobs have split shifts, and others have schedules that change from week to week or even day to day.

I have had students who were "on call" and in the middle of class they were called to come to work. They were always frustrated because they assumed that after their one-on-one discussion with their employers about their educational endeavors, they would never be called to work during class time. They left my class with sincere apologies and the promise to call another student to find out what they missed. They learned the hard way that "on call" included class time.

If going to college will affect some aspect of your job, you should consider getting an oral agreement with your employer about how to handle any time conflicts. (I doubt that you can get a written agreement but you are welcome to try.) You need to be prepared to offer suggestions on how to handle time conflicts. For example, you may be able to work a longer shift on another day or as some of my students have done, you may agree to return to work after class. On the other hand, do know that because classes are offered at various times from early morning until night, you have a pretty good chance of being able to take most of your classes around your work schedule. Every now and then one of your classes may only be held at the same time as your work hours; but this will be a rare event which is a point that should go over very well with your employer.

Whatever the case, it is your responsibility to make sure that your job and your college life exist in harmony. Missing work for class or missing classes for work will not create a stress-free college life. It is obvious how missing work days will affect your job with the worst case scenario being you get fired, but it might not be so obvious how missed classes can impact your education. No matter your level of intelligence, missed classes translate into missed learning which translates into poor grades.

As I write this, I have a student who is working for a company that encourages their employees to get a degree by providing full tuition reimbursement. The interesting thing is that this student has missed several of my classes already. She even missed two consecutive classes which for all intensive purposes is a week since my class only meets twice a week. When I had a discussion with her about her absences, I reminded her that there was a maximum amount of absences that she was allowed before it would be necessary to have her drop the course. She informed me that her employer had given her a promotion. I congratulated her and explained that her absences were still unexcused. While she insisted that her job firmly supported her going to college since they were paying her tuition; this same employer kept sending her out of town to work on different projects. Obviously, she could not be in two places at one time and her loyalty had to be to the one who was paying her tuition even though the one who was paying her tuition was the same one who was pulling her out of class. Go figure!

So what did she need to do? Keep everybody in the loop; that is, her employer and her professors. I allowed the aforementioned student to make up some of her assignments and suggested that she meet me during my office hours for further help. She also agreed to have another discussion with her employer because her grade average was already slipping due to her absences. Remember that the more your professors are aware of your circumstances (not in a way that you need to confess your personal life story), the more they can make informed decisions with regard to make-up work and individual tutoring. However, the professor has the right not to let you make up the work especially if your absences are outside of the guidelines stated in the syllabus.

Others. Besides family, friends, and employers, are there any other people in your life that you want to come on board to support you or to at least be aware that you are attending college? I really do not know but you do. It could be anybody from your neighbor to the cashier at the grocery store. If any of these people can be a source of support and inspiration for you, then why not let them know that you are going to college? When they see you, they will ask you "how's college life?" and you will be able to talk profusely about how excited you are to be getting an education. Just be sure that you carefully choose who you tell because I have learned from past experience that jealousy rears its ugly head and tries to stop you in your tracks when you least expect it.

Regardless of whom you tell and who supports you or not, you must become your number one cheerleader. What are the words to that song? "Don't let nobody tell you what you cannot do! Remember if you don't follow your dream, you'll never know what's on the other side of the rainbow."

Activity

Create a chart with the following headings: Family, Friends, and Employers. Make a list of the points you want to make with each group concerning your need to go to college. Your list should include why you intend to go to college, what kind of impact it will have on the group, and what kind of support you will need from each group. Do not make your list haphazardly. Complete your chart over several days so that you can make sure your list is comprehensive. Be creative and add more headings and any other information to the chart that you need.

5
Knowledge is the Key

I suspect that you are probably wondering why I would waste your time trying to convince you that "knowledge is the key" to reaching your future goals when you have already made the decision to go to college. Do not fret! I am not going to preach to the choir! The knowledge that I am talking about is beyond the four walls of the classroom. And no, I am not suggesting that you take additional classes beyond those on your home campus although (Don't you just love the word "although"?) taking a yoga or meditation class would definitely be beneficial to keeping you relaxed and positive. If there is such a class at your college, I encourage you to enroll in that class. If there is no such class, consider taking a class near your home or buying a video so you can practice in your home.

An excellent video that I use is *Yoga* by Wai Lana that you can order by going to the www.wailana.com on the Internet. But I digress. The knowledge that this chapter is focused on is the knowledge that comes from experiencing your campus outside of your immediate classes. I know what you are going to say. You barely have time to attend your classes, much less experience the campus, right? Your life is already overflowing with a job, family, friends, expenses, responsibilities, life's quirky surprises, traffic, weather, and now, homework. Most of you probably come straight from work to college and sometimes back to work, and when you do finally go home, you are overwhelmed with family, chores, running errands, and of course, homework. (I like saying, "homework.")

And I suppose, if you live in a dormitory on campus, your life is no picnic either. If it is your freshman year, you will be faced with being "independent and responsible." I remember the hardest thing about living on campus freshman year was that I had to personally do all those things that my mom used to do for me like wake me up in time to go to school, wash my clothes, prepare my meals (well not just for me but for the whole family), advise and help me with this and that—you get the picture. It was not until my first year in college that I truly realized that the biggest chore that I had done by myself when I was living at home was cleaning my bedroom. College forced me to take charge of my own life in ways I had taken for granted.

Whether you are full-time or part-time, living on campus or off campus, coming straight from high school or returning to college after years of being away—whatever your circumstance, you need to take time to explore and get comfortable with your campus. If your campus is located on city streets, know that your campus is the surrounding city. By making a "connection" with your college outside of the classroom, you increase your chances of a positive, more relaxed, and enjoyable college experience. You can also increase the quality and quantity time with your family and friends. Let me show you how.

Let's start with two of the most well-known buildings on campus: the bookstore and the cafeteria. Have you ever thought about using the bookstore for more than just buying books and the cafeteria for more than just eating food? Sounds like a strange question but really, it's not. The bookstore and the cafeteria have more to offer than just books and food respectively.

College bookstores sell a lot more than books and other

school supplies. You can find snacks, clothing, cards, stuffed animals, and other knick knacks. I always like buying t-shirts, sweat shirts, and jackets especially when they are on sale. Buying articles with the college's name on it can be inspirational as well as make nice gifts for family and friends. Gifts will help remind them that you are investing in a positive venture and will encourage them to be more supportive. Plus, you can always bring your family and friends to the bookstore to let them choose what they want to purchase. So, on a day when there is no long line of exhausted students trying to buy books, why not take time to browse and experience all that your bookstore has to offer?

And what about the benefits of the cafeteria? Why not meet with your family and friends for a snack or meal before or after class? Dare you even try to have a breakfast date before an early morning class? I am positive that if you have children, they will love the idea of meeting mommy or daddy at college for a campus meal. The cafeteria can also be your meeting place before you all go to the movies, the mall, or even stay for a campus event.

Whenever you do something fun right after class (not that going to class isn't fun) you will find that you will have a more enjoyable evening because you are allowing yourself some down time instead of heading toward your next responsibility. So every now and then, change your after-class routine. You can go to the cafeteria alone to enjoy your favorite cup of coffee and your own company. There will be times when what you need the most is time alone. You must take that time. You must never neglect yourself. Remember that you are just as important as everybody else in your life!

Now, the truth of the matter is that the bookstore and the cafeteria are just a small fraction of your campus. Regardless of how busy your life is, I really want to encourage you to little by little spend some quality time experiencing the lay-out of the rest of your campus; to be aware of the various organizations and activities; and to introduce yourself to new people. If you make this investment, you will create a win-win situation for yourself. Remember that it is your tuition that helps pay for this new fancy backyard of yours, so why not play in it? Take a personal tour of your campus or if you want historical facts and fun details, sign up for a formal tour with a campus guide. If time is an issue, set aside fifteen minutes before or after class, or take time during a class break to just walk around the campus. What are some of the other on-campus places that you should check out? Learn the locations of all the buildings with special emphasis on finding the administration, counseling, and security buildings. Also, be sure to seek out those buildings related to your field of study.

Find out who does what in the administration offices because they can be valuable resources for answering any questions you might have, for providing information about campus job opportunities, and for helping you with your future career endeavors. Sometimes it really is who you know that makes the difference. Keeping positive and friendly contacts can only work to your advantage.

Let me make one important point about the counseling office. You absolutely should spend quality time with your counselor/advisor each semester but know that you are ultimately responsible for making sure that you follow the curriculum outlined in the catalog of the year that you entered college. Always verify that you and your advisor are on the same page. Make sure you understand the sequence of courses for your program; and most importantly, make sure you keep a detailed record of your courses with copies of your final grades. Every now and then, a student cannot graduate because he or she missed taking just one course. So, please be meticulous about following your curriculum.

What's good about knowing where the security office is located? The main purpose of the security office is to protect campus personnel and property twenty-four hours a day. Basically, it is your on-campus police department. However, it is also the place where you register your car for campus parking; it is typically the place where the lost and found service is located; and it is the place where you can go for any personal emergencies. Stop by your security office and find out exactly what they offer and make sure you keep their phone number on hand.

After you get through your general education courses, the buildings related to your major are where you will spend a great deal of your time. Do not just pass by these buildings. Note the office hours of offices that are closed so that you can stop by in the future. Walk in and greet college personnel who have their office doors open. Introduce yourself. Engage in conversations and let the professors and department chairs know your aspirations. Find out if they can offer any advice on how to make it easier for you to reach your goals. Pick up fliers, pamphlets, and all written information that is valuable for you.

Don't forget to check out the location of the library. Ask for a personal tour, if you like. Besides books, you have access to all that computers offer, the latest magazines, various tapes and CD's—explore and learn. Your college library will have some special treats beyond that of your neighborhood public library. These treats include books, periodicals, visual aids, and other materials specifically geared to the college curriculum. Plus, sometimes different colleges work together and allow students from other colleges to have access to their books for a small fee. You usually need a consortium card for that library. (Consortium? Good word to look up if you are not sure). Your college librarian can help you with this. Learn the policies of the library and make friends with the librarians. Librarians are like walking encyclopedias or at the very least they know where those encyclopedias are located.

As an aside, it is a good idea to also have library cards from public libraries. Besides books and other materials, public libraries are great places to study. Most public libraries have a large room or several small rooms that are sound-proofed for quiet study.

Also, check out the physical education building. Note the information on the bulletin boards and see if there are any activities that you would be interested in. Is there a swimming pool? Your tuition also pays for the privilege of using the pool whether you are a physical education major or not. Take time to find out the hours that the pool is available for recreational use. If you do not know how to swim, this is as good a time as any to take a swimming class. Swimming is a great way to relieve stress while learning a life saving tool and building your body physically.

And is there a tennis court? How about a basketball court? Football field? Are you getting the picture yet? Look at your tuition and fees as paying for extracurricular activities that you may be able to enjoy without enrolling in the class. And it is not just about you. Find out about all the campus activities that are open to family and friends. Nearly every campus has a theatre department. Why not make sure that you and your family get to see plays during the semester? And what about national holidays like the Fourth of July? Maybe your campus will have its own fireworks' show. Of course, there will be a charge for some events but where your family and friends are concerned; it will be a good thing to make college a part of their lives as much as possible so that they will think of your campus as their campus. Now, if it is a case where you want to go to a college event alone, you may be able to volunteer to help out with the event and in turn, get to be at the event free of charge.

Well, I am not going to walk you through every building but at some point you should know your campus like the back of your hand. And if you do not know the back of your hand; well, that's another discussion. Knowing your physical campus will help you locate some *downtime* places. You will find yourself pleasantly surprised when you locate cozy areas where you can just plop down and read a good book, or possibly stare out over a lake, or hide out in solitude. Maybe you will find special walking paths. If your college is in the city know the locations of coffee shops, restaurants, theaters, and bookstores. Maybe on the weekend, your family and friends can join you for a campus-related walk. It is your campus. Why not show it off?

With regard to the human factor, making new friends with other students through activities and organizations will be a good thing as long as you carefully choose friends who are serious about college. Stay away from the party crowd because too many of them will "party" themselves right out of college! Since many students are employed full-time or owners of their own businesses, it is very possible that you will meet students who can help you in your future endeavors whether it is as a reference or as a new hire in their companies. You never know. Just keep in mind that networking with industrious students can be beneficial for all parties involved.

One last point, I promise. Getting through college with minimum stress requires a bit of work on your part. I use the word, "work," but really it has to do with a way of being. Be open to everything your college has to offer. In other words, make your tuition count for more than taking classes. One way to experience minimal stress in college is by enjoying your campus like it is your own backyard.

Activity

Get campus maps to give to your family members and friends. With regard to your immediate family, you can tape one map to the refrigerator or on the family bulletin board. Mark the locations and times of your classes on the map. Use the map when you take your family for a tour of the campus so that they have a three dimensional view in their minds. Be sure to mark the cafeteria, library and other meeting places.

6

Prepare for Your First Day

If you want your first day to be productive, enjoyable, and peaceful, you must prepare several weeks in advance. Do you remember preparing for your first day of elementary school? Most likely, your parents or guardians bought all your school materials in advance when stores were having their great "back to school" sales. I was lucky enough to be among the group of elementary kids who arrived on the first day with shiny new must-have items such as a lunch box with my favorite cartoon characters, a cool book bag, a couple of fat pencils, a box of fat crayons, a big eraser, and a pad of writing paper. I was also spoiled or should I say bribed (Believe it or not, I wasn't exactly excited about returning to school after summer break) with a brand new outfit and sometimes even a brand new pair of shoes. Thanks to my cool things and my cool outfit, I was excited about the first day of school mostly just to show off. (Of course, we outgrow *showing off* when we get older, right?)

What about bringing some of that same excitement to your first day at college? I really believe that all too often we take life way too seriously. Lighten up! Laugh more! Smile and add a cup of fun to your daily living. I read somewhere that even if you fake laughter, your body will respond positively because it will believe that you are sincerely laughing. So I now fake laughing when I am feeling down and the beauty of it is that I usually start laughing *for real* because my fake laughter is quite hilarious. *Seriously!* Just because you are an adult does not mean that you shouldn't do whatever it takes to make your first day more special. Of course, I know you can be happy without buying a new outfit but if you can afford it why not? But new outfit or not, do enjoy shopping for the following necessary learning supplies before your first day of class. Any other supplies that your professors require should be brought as soon as possible after the first day of class.

Basic learning supplies. If you want the most for your money, you should buy your supplies in bulk and on sale. Hint: A couple of weeks before elementary schools open for fall classes keep an eye out for sales on school supplies. There will be all kinds of back to school sales everywhere such that you will have your choice of shopping at several stores to get the best bargains.

Right now, my hall closet doubles as my supply closet and I have at least thirty spiral notebooks that I bought for ten cents each, ten packs of college-ruled loose-leaf paper that I bought for twenty-five cents each, and an assortment of pens, pencils, highlighters, and other supplies that I bought at ridiculously low prices. And guess what? I get my print paper free or discounted by turning in my used print cartridge to the office supply store. So, keep your eyes and ears open and you will be surprised at what deals you will run across.

Now what particular supplies should you purchase? Of course, you know to buy the obvious supplies: three-ring binders, spiral notebooks, college-ruled loose-leaf paper, highlighters, pens, pencils, a pack of paper clips, and a mini-stapler. The mini-stapler comes in handy when you have to turn in an assignment that is several pages long. I hate it when students fold the upper left corner of the pages down and rip the edge twice to keep the pages together. Paper clips are okay but a stapler guarantees keeping the papers together. If you have too many pages for a staple, then put them in a nice folder. Invest in a three-hole puncher or you can buy the cheaper one-hole puncher and use a sheet of notebook paper to line up the three holes. The hole puncher allows you to punch holes in all your hand-outs so that you can keep them neatly in your three-ring binders. Make sure you have extra paper and printer cartridges for your printer.

Post-its. Dare I mention "Post-its"? I have no stock in the company so my bias is strictly related to my personal usage. Post-its make wonderful book marks that do not fall out of place, great homework reminders that you can post on your computer screen, excellent snack deterrent reminders for your refrigerator door (late night studying promotes snacking), and useful reminders of what not to forget when you post them at eye level on your front door. I hate to sound like a commercial but once you use Post-its, it's hard to live without them.

File folders. Splurge and buy a large box of multi-colored file folders and you just might find yourself smiling every time you use them. The folders can be used to create a comprehensive filing system that includes lessons, graded papers, course grades, and any other materials valuable to your college future. (Know that your graded papers are your best proof if some unforeseen incident happens where your grades are in question. Yes, the burden of proof does fall on you.)

A dictionary and a thesaurus. First, the dictionary. You should have at least two dictionaries: a hardback dictionary that stays in your home and a nice pocket dictionary that you carry to your classes. Yes, electronic dictionaries are also fine. What is important to note is that the dictionary is too often underused in that students mainly use it for finding the definition and pronunciation of words. But a dictionary can provide so much more information about the word such as variant spelling, etymology, grammatical information, usage information, parts of speech, and abbreviations to name a few. Some dictionaries are even like mini-encyclopedias so get your money's worth by purchasing an excellent dictionary and using it to the fullest.

Second, the thesaurus. I cannot begin to tell you how valuable a tool a thesaurus is for students. Think about this. How many times have you had a word in mind to use but you knew that there was a better word that could make your explanation clearer? That's the job of a thesaurus. It's a great book of synonyms. For example, when I look up the word, "study," in my *New Roget's Thesaurus*, it not only provides synonyms but lists them according to the parts of speech. For the word, "study," a sample of the synonyms noted in the noun category is "learning, acquisition of knowledge, acquirement, attainment, scholarship, and erudition." A sample of the list of words in the verb category is "to learn, to acquire, gain, catch, receive, imbibe, pick up and gather." The list of words in the adjective category is "docile, apt, teachable, persuasible, and studious." What is really special about the thesaurus is that you only have to come up with one good word to find a host of others.

Why not take a stroll in the reference section of your favorite local book store? Do not buy just any dictionary or thesaurus. Study the lay-out, print size, illustrations, definitions, word lists, and other information. Choose the best dictionary and thesaurus that work for your needs.

A suitable book bag. A book bag, preferably one on wheels, is a must have item that you will need if you are taking more than one course. Nowadays, a book bag is an easy and efficient way to carry books, school supplies, and snacks. Do take time and carefully select a sturdy and spacious bag with enough compartments to best support your long term needs. Choose a color that you like but consider a color that does not show dirt easily.

When I got my first teaching job, I could not afford the prices of those fancy book bags so I bought a basic piece of luggage that only cost about ten dollars and had only one zipped compartment in the front. The wheels were extremely loud when I rolled it around campus because the wheels were made of hard plastic (as one of my students so eagerly pointed out). Whenever I wanted to retrieve my books and supplies, I had to lay it down flat to open it. No problem. It served my purpose.

Remember this! You do not have to buy into brand names or what everybody is wearing or doing. You are on campus for knowledge and the most knowledgeable people, at the very least, make decisions based on their needs as opposed to what society dictates is the latest fashion or must do. You are not in college to try to impress anyone or to be like anyone else! You are an individual trying to improve your life by gaining more knowledge and using it to your best advantage. The tools of the trade are your brain and your books so how you get them to the classroom is not as important as that you get them there. Having said that, the only reason that I eventually changed to a "real" book bag was because I had a little more money to invest and my new bag was way more convenient with the various compartments for bottled water, lunch, my supplies, and of course, my books. However, both book bags served their primary purpose of transporting my books and supplies so that my arms would not fall off.

Personal supplies. When you are looking for supplies, walk down the supply aisles of your local office supply store, your college book store, and your favorite retail store to see what other school supplies suit your personality. Think fun. Yes, fun! If you think a funny looking pen or rainbow-colored pencil will help you enjoy taking notes or completing your homework, then why not buy it? I have two cloth dolls, one in a bright red heart-designed outfit with a matching bonnet and shoes; and the other in a blue-checked outfit also with a matching bonnet and shoes. Both of them have big smiles on their faces as they sit on my printer which is next to my computer where I am sitting a great part of the day. They are sitting there facing me to remind me not to take myself too seriously. "Smile," they encourage with their own smiles as I try to incorporate a "light" attitude into the seriousness of this book. Whatever you do, especially when investing in an education, do it with seriousness, but also do it with love and joy. Life is too short for anything less.

Textbooks. Now, that you have the basic supplies, try to buy your textbooks before the first day of class. Remember not to write in them just in case your professors decide to use different texts. (Do you see the "not" in that sentence?) That way you can return them and get refunds. Note: If you are buying your books on-line make sure that the seller guarantees to have your books arrive by the time you need them. I have had students whose books did not arrive until a couple of weeks after class had begun. Be careful about buying used books especially when the answers are written in them because that will do you more harm than good. Yes, I am serious. You need to figure out your own answers. How else will you learn?

So what will you do with textbooks that you purchase before the first day of class? Become familiar with them, of course. How? Take the following steps with each book: First, peruse the table of contents. Second, survey the entire book so that you can get an overview of what the book is about. Flip through the pages stopping here and there to study pictures, captions, bold print, or an ant crawling across the page. Your primary goal in this survey is to get a feel for your book and learn a few things while you are at it. Third, read the introduction. (Please read the introduction.)

After you read the introduction, set aside some time to read the first three chapters. You do not have to read them in one sitting but do read them carefully before the first day of class. As you read, take notes on a separate sheet of paper. Let me reiterate one last time that just in case you have to return the book, you must *not* write in it until after the first day of class when you are absolutely sure that your professor will be using that book.

What should your notes for the first three chapters include? Include whatever you feel is important enough to commit to memory. If there are any words that you do not know, create a vocabulary list. Look up the definitions and then see if you can use the words in sentences. Also, if there is any information that you do not understand, create a list of questions. If any of your questions are not answered after your professor's lecture, then by all means ask your professor.

Know that by investing in reading a few chapters in your books ahead of time, you are helping to create a stress-free atmosphere for yourself.

Activities

Make a detailed list of the supplies that you need. For a comprehensive list, try to contact your professors by e-mail to see if there are supplies that are specific to their classes. Also, if you can reach your professors before the first class, it is as good a time as any to inquire about the specific books needed for their classes.

7
The Race is On

The first day has finally arrived. You barely slept last night, right? (Okay, maybe you have never gotten enough sleep on a regular basis because your extremely busy life forces you to burn the candle at both ends.) Maybe I should ask if your anxiousness about your first day affected your sleep. Even today, I am still a little anxious the night before the first day regardless of whether I will be in the role of student or the role of professor.

So what causes first day anxiety? It is very logical, really. You have no knowledge of what the first day is going to be like. Will parking be a piece of cake or a nightmare? Will your professor be easy or strict or just right? (Remember Goldie Locks testing out the chairs in *The Three Bears*?) Will your classmates be friendly or snobbish or apathetic? Will you fit in or do you even want to fit in? Will there be tons of homework? (Well, I hope so.) Have I created stress and presented questions that never crossed your mind? If so, forgive me. The point I am trying to make is that it is very normal to have some anxiety about any new undertaking. Whether you are going to college for the first time, returning after years of being away, or starting the first day of a new term, every first day is still a "new" day that you have yet to experience.

The good news is that the first day and future days will all come together in a very positive way if you stay focused on your capacity to be a model student. Professor Nader Angha, the world renowned Sufi Master and author of many books including *Theory I: The Unlimited Vision of Leadership*, notes that leadership is "the creative capacity to evoke the most positive capabilities and potentialities within ourselves, and consequently, within others" (p. 168). My point is that anxiety will not take hold of your college days if you are about being and acting in college according to your "capabilities and potentialities" as opposed to what family, friends, and society dictate. You have to be the unique individual that you were created to be and not worry about outside forces. Sometimes the most distracting outside force is other students.

Ask yourself what impact will the other students have on your education? Unfortunately, sometimes college becomes a place where students forget their individuality and try to fit in. They become the third grader influenced by peer pressure; but as I always say to myself, I say to you now, "You are too mature to respond to peer pressure." Plus, college is about expanding your knowledge not about limiting your choices. Even in something as mundane as dressing, you must dress according to your preference and comfort.

When I first started teaching college, many of the other female professors were dressed in their Sunday best, if you will, with the appropriate high-heeled shoes. I, on the other hand, had no intention of prancing around campus in my Sunday best and especially not in my high-heeled shoes. I chose to wear casual clothes and my feet enjoyed the comfort of tennis shoes. For me, I could be a much better professor when it did not matter if I got chalk on my clothing and when my feet were flat on the ground. (Now, as I write this, I can say I dressed to be grounded and I still do today). I avoid high-heeled shoes like the plague. Of course, my point is only to say to dress according to what makes you comfortable and if that is high-heeled shoes, then so be it. As the saying goes,

"To each, his own." (But why are women still wearing high-heeled shoes when they know it puts the future of healthy feet and ankles in jeopardy?)

First and foremost, your first day and every other day at college are about you being the master of your body, mind, and soul. (Actually, this is how you should always live your daily life.) Dressing for college success means that you dress so that your focus will be on learning. Be comfortable. (Do I have to say that wearing a bathing suit to class is a little too comfortable?) Be comfortable in all aspects of whom you are and that includes bringing a bag lunch if you don't want to spend money in the cafeteria or hit the vending machines. To this day, I still take a sandwich, snack, piece of fruit, and a bottle of water for lunch. Actually, it is not only cheaper but healthier. Although you will see many students walking around campus with expensive cups of coffee in their hands, you can always bring your coffee from home in a thermos bottle. I sometimes bring hot tea.

There are no college rules that I know of that require you to change who you are to get an education. Show up to get the knowledge that you are paying for in both time and money. And after you show up, the way to maintain peace of mind is to be an open-minded individual with a strong will to learn. Now, let me give you seven important habits for the first day that will serve you throughout your college education.

1. Stay focused. Not only on the first day but from this day on, you will have to learn to control your wandering mind so that you can give your full attention and concentration to the lesson. The funny thing is that all too often once your professor starts talking your mind will wander to every other subject besides the subject at hand. You might find yourself thinking about all the things you need to do when you get out of class such as running errands, planning dinner, or going back to work. Everything and anything that has nothing to do with the lesson will cross your mind.

What is the way to get your mind under control? First, be aware of what you are thinking about. Second, find a phrase that works for you like "not now" that allows you to gently push your thoughts aside and stay focused. Third, inhale deeply and exhale slowly as you refocus to the present. Remember that you have plenty of time to think about the issues in your life later. Your time in the classroom requires focusing on the lesson.

I always tell my students to leave all their problems at the door and come into my classroom with a clear mind, an empty slate, if you will. I assure them that they can pick up their problems on the way out when the class is over.

2. Take notes. I do not know why some students think the first day is only supposed to be about finding the classroom and meeting the professor. Actually, the first day is about much more. The first day sets the tone for what the rest of the classes are going to be like so after the introductory material is presented, your professor will most likely teach. I know I always do! I try to give my students their money's worth. You should be prepared with all your supplies: paper, pens, highlighters, and of course, your books. Take detailed notes. Ignore your brain when it tells you that you can remember everything without writing it down. If you are like so many students, your life is already full, so why put one more thing on your mind. Take correct and intelligible notes so that besides your homework, you have information that you can review and act on later.

3. Ask questions. Of course, ask a million and one questions if you have to because your tuition pays for that professor who is standing before you. Your professor is there to serve you with regard to knowledge and if you do not understand something, you need to ask because believe it or not, most professors are not mind readers. (There are only a few of us left who read minds but we usually only read minds on Tuesdays and Thursdays.)

Believe me, you will not be the only one with that same question, and if by chance, you are—then good for you! I only ask that you have paid good enough attention to the lecture so that you are not asking a ridiculous question. A ridiculous question is when you ask a question that was already clearly answered by your professor while you were off daydreaming instead of being in the present moment.

4. Study the syllabus. So you have got the first day down pact but what about the next class day as well as the weeks to come. How do you insure peace and tranquility with all the studying ahead of you? You begin with the syllabus that your professor hopefully handed to you on the first day of class. (If you did not get it on the first day, you should definitely have it by the next class.) The worst thing that you can do with the syllabus is to glance at it and tuck it away never to look at it again. The very best thing that you can do with the syllabus is to study it. I am not kidding! Your personal homework assignment should be to actively read the syllabus from beginning to end in one sitting. Use your highlighter and take notes directly on the syllabus.

Highlight the time and location of your professor's office hours. Note all the ways you can contact your professor. If there is no contact information, ask your professor to provide contact information. Make sure you understand all the rules about tardiness, absenteeism, and assignment deadlines. Be clear about how assignments are graded. Highlight important dates of quizzes, tests, and of course, the final exam. Write any questions that you might have in the margin of the syllabus and ask those questions at the next class meeting. Preview your textbook(s) with regard to the chapters noted on the syllabus and set up a schedule whereby you can preview or even read the chapter(s) before the lecture.

5. Create contacts. What else should you do in those first couple of weeks? Make sure you get at least three of your classmates' phone numbers and/or e-mail addresses by the end of the second week of class. You need to be able to get in touch with a classmate if you are absent to find out what you missed so that you will be prepared as much as possible when you return. Another reason for getting contact information with other classmates is for forming a study group. If you connect with serious students, a study group can be very beneficial. You just have to make sure the group is about studying and not socializing. Study time needs to be strictly honored. After one meeting, you will know if everybody is on the same page as you. If your study group is not about studying, then find another study group if you feel the need to join one. Personally, study groups never worked for me. I like studying alone or with one other person. (Two is enough of a crowd for me.)

Of course, I must note that when I say I like studying alone, that a lot of my studying during my doctorate was done in coffee shops and libraries. A few times during that period I arranged to meet another student to study with in those same coffee shops and libraries. Interestingly enough, we were not in the same field. We were also going to different colleges but found that we could study longer if it was the two of us. We would meet at preset times and study silently for one hour or so before we took a ten minute break. Then we would dive back into our studies. We truly took advantage of late hour study sessions like meeting at a coffee shop or one of our homes at 10:00 at night. What was interesting was that we were competitive in studying and found ourselves fighting back sleep sometimes until 2:00 in the morning. I really enjoyed those study sessions. Yes, I did! Of course, burning the midnight oil is not for everyone.

6. Do your homework. Can I talk about homework for a minute? Please, do not miss any homework assignments. There is nothing else to say about that. It is called homework for a reason so I wonder why so many students try to do their homework assignments right before the class on the day when it is due. What you need to remember is that homework is the way for you to find out what you know and what you don't know. It shouldn't be a rush job. Just do it with love, eagerness, and diligence. And if you have any problems, see your professor. And please, please turn all your assignments in on time. What is the best way to do that? Do not wait until the last minute! So simple, and yet, we as professors will always get the excuse that an assignment is late because of an emergency the night before the due date. There is a major problem with such an excuse when the assignment was given weeks in advance.

7. Get help. See your professor during office hours if you need some one-on-one help. That's why they are called office hours—they are hours in the office that you can meet with your professor one-on-one. (Sorry professors, I have also used those many office hours for writing lesson plans, grading papers, and sipping a cup of tea because students rarely showed up.) Now, please be clear about my next point. The office hours are not set up for you to tell your life story or present all your personal issues. You need to see a therapist for that. The office hours are so that your professor can help you with the subject matter. It allows you to get one-on-one help from the person who is actually teaching the subject.

Don't forget the tutorial center! You can also get additional help from tutors on campus. They are usually open a minimum of six days a week with hours that should even match your busy schedule. You see, college is truly set up so that you will have all the necessary resources to succeed. So why not take advantage of what you have already paid for?

Activities

The night before your first day, sit for a minimum of twenty minutes doing your deep breathing exercises. Make sure to go to bed early enough to get a good night's rest and get up early enough to enjoy a healthy breakfast. If your class is after work, make sure you have a healthy snack or meal before class. Do try to get on campus early enough to calm down from the day before your class starts.

8
Stay Organized

Staying organized is not only necessary for minimizing stress in your college life but it will also help you minimize stress in every part of your life. Think about it for a moment. You will quickly realize that you are definitely getting more than your money's worth in this chapter. However, before we look at the value of organization, let me first respond to those doubting students who believe that organization wastes valuable time.

I always get some students who shun organization like it is a contagious disease. I remember the verbal battering one of my students got from her classmates when she said that her socks were not only organized according to color and length but also according to the season. It was a given that she had each sock paired with its mate. Some students insisted that all she needed to do was pair a sock with its mate and throw them in the drawer. Some of them even insisted that any drawer would do as opposed to a drawer dedicated to socks only.

Be that as it may, consider how long it takes you (the one who is unorganized) to find a pair of socks to match your outfit on a given day. "Just a couple of minutes," you say proudly. Well, multiply, let's say, two minutes by 365 days in a year and consider how much better it would have been to have been spending those 12 hours and 10 minutes practicing your deep breathing exercises or sipping a cup of your favorite herbal tea. (Okay, you could have been drinking a cup of your favorite coffee.) Now, if you feel that the example about the socks is beneath you (couldn't resist that), let me use an example that we all can relate to—the "I can't find my keys" scenario.

So how many times in your life have you (again, I am talking to those of you who are unorganized) had to take time out of your busy life to search for your keys before you left the house? Did it take you five minutes or longer? Did you enjoy playing hide and seek with your keys? Of course not. I do not think there is anyone who would not prefer to just grab their keys and go. So why not just invest in a key holder or put your keys in the same place every single time? Yep, it is as simple as that! It really is! The problem is that too often your mind is busy with a million other things when you enter your home. Where you put the keys becomes a non-issue; that is, until you have to leave the house again. If you work on keeping your mind in the present, you will minimize wasted time and effort. Buying a key holder and placing it near the path you always take when you enter your home is one way to fix the lost key syndrome.

When I have suggested purchasing a key holder to students who had already spent years searching for their keys, this solution always worked. The major problem was that it took them a long time to buy the key holder because they would always forget to buy it. Simple solution. Add "purchase a key holder" to your To Do list. You do have a To Do list, don't you? Geez! Well, To Do list or not, you need to keep a College To Do list. At the very least, this list should include needed supplies and homework assignments with due dates on a calendar or in a day planner dedicated to your college work.

What other items should be on your College To Do list? You might consider having a list of "things to do" when you arrive on campus each day. This list might include going to the library to check out or return books, making copies, reviewing your notes, stopping by any offices, or meeting with professors. You certainly do not have to put buying a snack on the list because you do not need to be reminded of that, right? But if you have several tasks to take care of once you arrive on campus, make a list and check each item off as you do them. Once you put the items on paper, you will have one less thing on your mind. I personally keep my College To Do list in a steno notebook in my book bag. I check off each item as I complete it. If at the end of the day there is an item that I did not get to, I rewrite it on the next page so that it is at the top of my list for the next time.

Okay. There is no down side to organization. Organization helps you live your life more efficiently. You actually gain more time and you manage your tasks with minimum stress. You have the added bonus of feeling good because you can actually see the positive effects that being organized has on your life. So focus on being organized in (1) your classes, (2) your study area, and (3) your personal life. Let me say ahead of time that, of course, organization will require that you invest some up-front quantity and quality time but trust me; it will be well worth it. Once you are organized, staying organized is a breeze—a wonderful, gentle, autumn breeze that makes handling college responsibilities so very much easier.

Your Classes

You must start organizing from the very first day of class and you must be vigilant about staying organized throughout your college life. Wake up call: You will accumulate a lot of paper in college and it will be your responsibility to keep your papers organized and easily accessible. What paper? Prepare yourself for an accumulation of quizzes, tests, and hand-outs; informational fliers from college-wide offices and organizations; advertising information created to lure college students to do one thing or another; and educational junk mail.

What is educational junk mail? I define educational junk mail as any material that is not pertinent to my subject area, my students, or me. (But understand that what is educational junk mail for me might be priority mail for somebody else.) When I go to my office mailbox, I grab everything out of the box and stand over the nearest trash can. As I sort through the mail, I throw away my educational junk mail. I am not kidding. This is a fast and efficient way to get rid of educational junk mail.

Not only that but I immediately skim each piece of mail that I have not labeled as educational junk mail and throw away anything that requires no further action except that I digest it. For example, there might be a flier detailing an upcoming lecture that would benefit me. I write the pertinent information in my planner, and then trash the flier. And for those materials that I decide to retain, I go one step further and decide where to file them. For example, I keep a folder in my book bag labeled information. This is for hand-outs that I need to refer to now and then throughout the semester like departmental information, exam schedules, and campus events. If a flier has information that I need to relay to my students, I put the notice in the folder related to that class so that I will not forget to tell them. Do you get the picture? The point is to immediately trash educational junk mail, and then to file or trash all other mail immediately. This way nothing piles up.

As your professors hand you materials on the first day and throughout the term, being organized requires that you make quick decisions about what to do with these materials. Of course, if the material is closely related to the lesson, that's a no brainer. Keep it until the last day of class. But suppose you were handed a flier that informs you of an upcoming campus event. You can trash it if you know you definitely are not going; place it in a folder or on your personal bulletin board for future reference if you plan to go; or write it down in your planner and then trash the flier. Are you starting to see all the benefits of taking immediate action?

Your next task is to efficiently manage whatever materials you decide to keep. Focus on the tests, quizzes, and homework assignments that you receive on a regular basis. Each class will have its own set of materials, so it will be necessary to keep the materials for each class separate and organized. One way to organize your materials is to organize them by category and date. For example, for each class, you can keep your graded papers in chronological order in one folder; all hand-outs from your professor in another folder; and your notes in a spiral notebook. Unless, your professor suggests otherwise, you should take notes for each class in separate spiral notebooks instead of buying a huge spiral notebook that has dividers.

Do you know some of the advantages of using separate notebooks? One is if you are unlucky enough to lose your notebook, you will be losing information from one class and not from all of your classes. But that's a negative. The other reason is to physically separate the information for each class for filing purposes at the end of the semester. Separate notebooks also allow you to take only what you need for that specific class which in turn creates a lighter book bag.

Something else that I have found that aids in organizing different class materials is using a color scheme. A color scheme has the double benefit of being pleasant to look at and being an excellent organizational tool. For instance, I use a red binder, red spiral notebooks, and red folders for one class; and a green binder, green spiral notebooks, and green folders for another. I can easily pull out the right materials from my book bag just by looking at the color. Now, if you are not impressed with my color coordination, it won't hurt my feelings; it is up to you to find creative ways to separate materials from different classes.

So where will you keep all these materials once you have everything organized? Well, you can go as formal as a file cabinet or as informal as boxes. Now, if you have a file cabinet you might consider using a different drawer for each class until that semester is over, and then putting all those classes for that semester in one drawer. If you use a box, it is easy to create dividers out of poster board. Use the dividers to separate each class's information. If the outside of the box is unsightly, you can dress it up with decorative contact paper.

When the classes for that semester are over, put all the materials for each class in a large envelope with the name, and beginning and ending dates of the class. You do not have to keep everything, but do be sure to keep all your graded papers until you have your final grade report. Also, make sure you keep all of your final grade reports until you graduate. All of your grade reports should be kept together in one place in chronological order.

Now once you start organizing, little by little you are going to start getting in the mood for organization. You will like being able to put your hands on what you want when you want it. When you become really good at organizing, it will spill over into your everyday life. Can you imagine how wonderful it will be to find what you are looking for the first time and every time? Do not imagine. Experience it. Besides all your paperwork, what else needs to be organized?

Your Study Area

The most important qualities of a study area are that it is clean, bright, organized, and inviting. It should be a place where your brain knows that the second you enter that space you are there for serious work. No ifs, ands, or buts about it, you know when you walk into your study area you have no option but to put your body in a chair and do the necessary work.

Where should this study area be located? If you have an actual "study" to study in, that's fine and dandy; however, it is okay if your study area is your bedroom, a closet, or even a corner of the kitchen table. It is even "A" okay if you have to leave your house and go to another place to study. Again, what is more important than location is that wherever you study, whether it is one place or several places, your mind and body are trained to know that when you are in that place, your full attention will be given to studying.

Just as an aside, I have had students tell me that there were so many people in their house that even if they could find a corner to study in, it would have been way too noisy for them to concentrate. Well, I have two suggestions if you have a similar problem. If you feel that you must stay in the house to study your last choice room could be in the bathroom with the exhaust fan on. You are bound to find some privacy there. Yes, I'm serious. Or if the weather is great, set up a study area on a blanket in the backyard.

Your neighborhood library might prove to be a great place to study. Most libraries have quiet rooms or sound proof cubicles if you are the kind of person who needs absolute quiet to study. You could also go to your own college library. If noise does not bother you, other places are homes of neighbors, friends, and other family members; coffee shops, sandwich shops, and park benches—well, just seek and you will find places that match the environment that you require for study. I have no doubt about that. You might even meet a good study partner along the way.

Okay, now let me add an "out of the box" comment about where you study. Try to match your study areas with your personality. If you are the kind of person that does not like change, then maybe you need to go to the exact same place all the time to be productive. But if you get bored early and need variety, you will require more variety in your places of study. My designated study/research/writing areas in my home include the desk in my bedroom; a room that I designate as my home office where I have two long tables, a computer, printer, fax, books and all sorts of writing materials; and my balcony on good weather days. My designated study/research/writing areas that I have to drive to include public libraries, parks, and coffee shops that are located in bookstores because I love perusing the books when I take a break.

I have a favorite bookstore/coffee shop that I love to frequent but because I have become friends with some of the employees over the years, I have to frequent it less and less. Friends are definitely a distraction. They forget that I have come there to work and not socialize, and because I enjoy their company so much, I forget to tell them. Regardless of which of the aforementioned places I go to, I know that I am there for serious work, not goofing off. (Well, I have already explained about the coffee shop). You will recognize your best places for study rather quickly, trust me. Better yet, trust yourself.

Once you have decided where you plan to study, and tested which places allow you to be more productive; there are some necessary study tools that should always be in your study area. If it is a room or area in your house your study tools should always be there. If it is a place that you have to travel to, then you should make a "study tools' bag." The study tools' bag should have the necessary writing implements such as paper, Post-its, paper clips, pens, and any other supplies you deem necessary. If you are using a study tools' bag, it should always be packed with the aforementioned supplies so that all you have to do is grab the bag and go. Of course, for some of you, your study tools' bag may be represented by your computer. Whatever works for you, go for it!

The possible downside of having more than one study area in your home is that each area really should have the basic supplies. I also try to keep an inspirational item in each area; for example, on one of my desks, I keep my writing implements in a cup, which says on one side, "Success is loving what you do" and the other side, "Success is doing what you love." Even though, I do have a computer and a printer in one of my study areas (not too many of us can have a computer and printer in each study area), I usually write poetry and even this book in long hand first before I go to the computer. I create better in long hand. After the first draft, I key in the information.

Some of the other supplies that I have in my study areas are dictionaries, thesauruses, calendars, file folders, staplers, highlighters, and desk clocks. I am very time-oriented and I always want to be aware of how long it is taking me to get something done. Make sure all of your supplies are organized on your desk for functionality. Of course, I have to take my books and other class-related materials from one study area to another. When I work on my balcony, I have to take my study tools' bag.

Now, here is my food and drink advice. Meals should be eaten before or after you study; however, it is okay to have tea, water, coffee, or some other non-alcoholic refreshment. Snacks like nuts, raisins, or candy are also okay. I keep a candy jar filled with a variety of hard candies on my desk. Again, suit your taste as long as what you are eating does not become more important than studying. Also, make sure that you go to the bathroom before you sit down so that you do not have an excuse to get up before you spend some quality time studying. As a writer, the standard rule for finishing a project is "keep your derriere in the chair." This is the hardest part of any assignment. You cannot even begin if you do not stay seated. If you are not careful, your brain will give you a million and one reasons to get up. Once you sit, commit to sitting for at least forty-five minutes before getting up. Then make sure you are re-seated within fifteen minutes.

Now, when I leave my house to study in a coffee shop or library, I have my study tools' bag along with my books. I try to make sure to always keep change in my purse to make copies if I need to and oftentimes, I carry bottled water. (Some libraries do allow coffee or water as long as it is in a closed container.) If you are organized from the beginning, most of your time will be spent studying instead of looking for things. Now that you have organized your classes and your study area, you are done, right? Not quite.

Your Personal Life

None of the aforementioned organization information will work efficiently if your personal life is a mess. There is no way to keep your personal life completely separate from your college life so you need to work on getting your personal life organized also. The more organized your personal life is, the more stress-free your college life will be. What parts of your personal life will impact your college life? Everybody and everything at any moment in time. Okay, I can make your world smaller. What about the people that live in the same house with you? For those of you who live alone, you can just read this passage with a content look on your face. (Now remember having a pet is not living alone. Trying to get a cat to honor your study time is like—well, you know.) Anyway, you need to sit down with paper, pencil, and a calendar to organize family activities so that they do not interfere with your study time.

The bottom line for some of you might be that your study time will have to happen when everybody is asleep. That might mean that you have to stay up and study after eleven at night or go to bed and get up early to study before your family awakens. It can be done. I know because I have taught those students.

Whatever the nature of your daily routine, as much as possible, try to set aside the same time to study and if it works for you, the same place to study. Making study time a habit will make your life easier in the long run. If there are other family members who are in school, you might be able to have family study sessions where family members are doing their homework at the same time that you are doing yours. When they see your smile and how positive you are about doing your homework; they might be more eager to do their homework.

The bottom line is that you must get you personal life in order so that it will not have a negative impact on your college life. It will require compromise and detailed planning in some cases but in the long run, it will be worth it to have a specific block of unencumbered study time. You are the one who is responsible for making sure that you have the time and space to study.

Activities

Act on the information provided in this chapter. Dedicate some time to specifically create a study area where you will enjoy the space and be productive. Do not get discouraged if your space is the size of a closet or the closet itself. Some of the top selling authors in the country have produced best-selling books from spaces that are no bigger than a closet. Make the space your own. Decorate it. Be creative! For more help on organizing, go to the following website: www.lifeorganizers.com

9
Reach for the Moon

Before I tell you about the five-year plan, I need to explain why I have chosen five years. The five-year plan covers the one year after you graduate with a four-year degree. However, if you are getting a two-year degree, then you should adjust this plan to a three-year plan. In other words, whatever the length of your college stay, you should create a plan that goes one year beyond you receiving your degree. So whenever I say "five-year plan" from this point on, you know that the number of years for your plan should be how long it takes to get your degree plus one year.

So what exactly is a five-year plan? First and foremost, it is a written goal setting plan that requires you to make some decisions on (1) exactly what you want from your college experience and (2) how you plan to get what you want. Why is it necessary to write it down? It is necessary because writing or printing it from the computer increases actualization; that is, putting your plan on paper brings your goals into the material world. Once your goals have moved from your mind to the material world of paper, you have taken your first step to actualizing them.

Your goals must be written in such a way that you can track

your progress and make adjustments as necessary. The most wondrous thing is that by tracking your goals, you are more able to lead a stress-free college life. Tracking your goals lets you know whether you are on schedule with accomplishing what you want to accomplish. If you are not, then you know immediately that some changes have to be made. Tracking your goals also lets you know where you need improvement. If improvement is needed you can then set very specific guidelines on how to improve whether it is by studying more, seeing your professor during office hours, seeing a tutor, or all of the aforementioned suggestions. Tracking your goals will also show you whether you can do more than you are already doing or whether you have overextended yourself and need to cut back.

So how do you write these goals? The foundation of your five-year plan will be made up of SMART goals. By using the common acronym in goal setting, SMART, you can create a five-year plan that contains the essential elements of goal writing. There are several variations on what each letter in SMART stands for so I am choosing the variation that best suits the needs of college students.

The "S" in SMART stands for *specific*. You need to make sure that the wording of your goals is very specific. Let's look at your first year of college. What is it that you specifically hope to accomplish in the first year? Of course, you want to pass all your courses but being specific requires that you state the specific grade you want to earn in each course. Besides the grade, you should state what your learning objectives are for each class. For example, in an English class, your goal might be to improve your knowledge of English grammar rules. You might state specifically that you want to memorize the rules for expressing future time.

The "M" in SMART stands for *measurable*. What good is a goal if you can't measure it? Well, I will tell you. It is worthless! You have to make sure that your goals are measurable so that you will know whether you are moving toward them or not. Of course, if your goal is to get all A's for all your courses at the end of the term, the measurement is easy. However, to make sure that you have an

"A" average in each class, you need to keep a running average of your grades to see if you are maintaining that "A" average. If you make a low grade on an assignment, you will immediately know how that grade affects your average. So your stated goal might say, "Whenever I receive a 'B' or lower, I will re-average all my grades to determine the impact of the new grade."

What I do need to mention is the "zero" effect. Let's say for some reason you do not turn in one of your assignments and as a result, you receive a zero for your grade. Let's say at this point you only have 3 grades so far; that is, 100, 100, and 0. What is your average? It is 66.6% which as you can see really tears down your used-to-be "A" average. This is the zero effect. So now what do you do?

The "A" in SMART stands for *action-oriented*. So you messed up and got a zero. What now? There are two questions that you need to ask yourself. First, what action can you take to make sure that you never get another zero? Second, what action can you take now that you have the zero? Let's address the first question. Since most zeroes are a result of not turning in an assignment, you need to put forth safeguards in your life to make sure that you turn in assignments on time. One safeguard is to keep a calendar of due dates for all assignments. Make sure you check the calendar daily. Another safeguard is to complete the assignment before the due date. I would suggest you complete assignments at least three days before the due date so that you are not impacted by any last minute emergencies like personal illness, family issues, or printer problems.

Now, for the second question. What action can you take now that you have the zero? Consult with your professor to see if there is something you can do like an extra credit assignment to remove that zero from your grades. Whether you are allowed the privilege of make-up work or not, your next action is to list what you need to do to insure that you get A's on the rest of your assignments. (Remember, I am talking about students who are determined to keep an "A" average.) Your list might include having a study partner, getting a tutor, and creating pre-tests before the actual test.

The point is to do whatever it takes and never give up. Do not let a zero or any low grade make you lose hope. Always stay hopeful and back up that hope with action.

The "R" in SMART stands for *realistic*. Yes, you should always want the highest grades but you need to ask yourself if getting an "A" average in all of your classes is realistic for you. Let me assure you that I am a firm believer that you can pretty much accomplish anything that you want to accomplish. The question is whether you have the willingness, the time, the resources, the perseverance, and the right attitude to accomplish your goals. Are you ready to do whatever it takes? If you are and you do, then there is every possibility that there will be an "A" knocking at your door.

The "T" in SMART stands for *timed*. Goal setting requires that you have a start date and an end date. Of course, the time is already set for you with regard to getting an "A" average because your start date is the first day of class and your end date is the day of the final exam. But what about trying to finish a paper with a six week deadline? You will need to divide the paper according to specific work required and set due dates to get the work done. For example, you could by the end of week two, make sure you have completed all the research; by the end of week four, you could have your first draft completed; by the end of week five, you could have finished your rewriting, updating, and fine tuning; and during the final week, you should have a final read through to make sure you have a perfect paper.

Besides weekly deadlines, you need to set daily goals to insure that you reach your weekly goals. I am not kidding. For example, your first week's daily goals for doing your research should be as specific as "I will spend Mondays, Tuesdays, and Wednesdays in the library from 5:00 P. M. until 8:00 P. M. doing research. From 8:30 P. M. until 10:00 P. M., I will hang out at the coffee shop to read and organize my notes." The key is the more detailed and specific you make your schedule, the easier it will be to follow it.

Now that you are clear on how to write your SMART goals, you need only to incorporate your SMART goals into a five-year plan. Of course, the foundation of your plan will always be the courses you plan to take each term. So create a chart each term with the following columns: (1) Courses; (2) Grades; (3) Knowledge; and (4) Plan of Action.

The first column requires that you list all the courses that you plan to take that term. With regard to your courses, you should verify that you are on the right track by checking your college catalog and consulting with your counselor. Of course, you are welcome to take courses that are of interest to you and have nothing to do with supporting your certificate or degree. The second column requires that you list the grades that you want to earn in those courses. Now, with regard to grades, we all want to make straight A's but is that a realistic goal for you if, for example, you have always barely passed your classes in high school. Is a "B" a more realistic goal for you? Please know that I am never saying that you can't make an "A" because I believe that no matter your past, if you want to make straight "A's" you can. You just need to be clear that going from a "D" to an "A" may require blood, sweat, and tears. On the other side of the fence, do not set your goals so low that it requires little action from you. Your goals should be reasonably challenging. So not to belabor the point, you should write the grade that you want to work toward for each class.

The third column is titled, "Knowledge." What is it that you hope to get from each class? Study the objectives for the class that your professor has noted in the syllabus. Are there some objectives that stand out for you more than others? Is there an objective that is not on the syllabus that you personally want to accomplish? Whatever it might be, you should in the knowledge column write a sentence that begins with "I want to learn . . ." and be very specific. List as many objectives as you deem necessary.

What plan of action do you intend to take to realize your preferred grades and your stated objectives? I have already talked about "smart goals" so you already know how to state your plan of action; that is, make it very detailed. A plan of action might include several steps. Maybe it does not need saying but the steps in your plan of action are to insure that you obtain the knowledge necessary to easily pass the course.

After you have listed all your courses and the appropriate information for those courses, on a separate page write, "Extracurricular Activities." Remember, there is a lot to do in college besides going to class. Are there some on-campus or off-campus college-related organizations that you want to be involved with? Make a list, update it each semester, and respond to the following questions for each organization. When would you like to join? What are the membership requirements for each organization and if you do not meet the requirements, what is your plan of action to meet them? What role do you want to play in that organization whether it is holding a particular office or doing something specific as a member of the organization? Do not forget to always write your "plan of action" using SMART goals.

I am hopeful that you get the general picture of what your four-year plan will look like; that is, for every term you will list new courses (you are not planning to repeat any, are you?) and the necessary related information. You will delete or add to your list of "Extracurricular Activities" as needed. You should create your chart at the beginning of each term. You should put your chart somewhere where you will see it on a regular basis so that you can make sure you are on track. You will probably find yourself updating your plan of action for some items as you move through your courses. There is nothing wrong with that. The plan of action is not written in stone.

Now, let's focus on that fifth year. You should definitely create the plan for your fifth year on paper before the actual fifth year; that is, write up your fifth year plan during your third year or at the top of your fourth year of college. The fifth year is directly related to what you plan to do with your degree when you graduate. It might be that you plan to continue your education by getting a higher degree and in that case, you should create a new plan with SMART goals. But if your plan is to find a job, then you need to have begun your research for the type of job you are looking for such that your fifth year chart should contain a list of specific places where you want to work; a brief synopsis of each job that includes contacts with locations, website addresses, and other contact information; and your deadline dates for sending resumes. For many companies you can send your resume within six months of your graduation date.

One way to get your foot in the door of a company before your graduation is to see if there is an internship program that you can get into while you are still in your third or fourth year of college. If you turn out to be a great intern, I do not see any reason why you would not be the first in line for full employment. If there is no internship program, consider volunteering a few hours a week while you are in your fourth year of college. (Yep, this is another way to get your foot in the door.)

Make sure the details are as specific and comprehensive for the fifth year as you made them for the other years of your plan. If there is only one specific company that you have always wanted to work for you might include the following information in your fifth year plan. Do your research and keep notes on important information about that company. Drop your resume off in person and get any brochures or information that you can get from the front office. While you are there, look at how people are dressed, how they talk, how they conduct themselves. Then visualize yourself working there and what you need to do to fit into that culture. Be overly prepared for your interview by practicing with friends and/or family members.

Do whatever is necessary to get the job but if you don't get it, you can always work somewhere else and apply again in a year or so. I know a professor who applied three consecutive years at her favorite college before she was hired. She refused to give up because that was the college where she preferred to teach. (Yes, I know that sometimes we have to let go and move on but first apply and apply and apply). However, before you reapply, very politely find out from the interviewer what you have to do to be a potential employee. It might just be that you have to hone your interviewing skills. Whatever it is, persevere and turn your weaknesses into strengths. Breathe deeply while you are at it!

Activity

Your activity is a no-brainer. You know what you need to do. Create a plan that is one year beyond your college stay. Make sure the plan follows the specific information provided in this chapter. Don't be shy about adding your own special touches.

10
A Potpourri of Do's and Don'ts

I want to make one final point. Well, ten more points to be exact. There was no way that I could end this book with a typical chapter any more than I could begin it that way. So I sat down and really thought hard about what it was that kept me moving forward in one college after another to accumulate five degrees with enthusiasm in spite of some really huge bumps in the road that I had to climb over or flatten. After pondering for several days, I came up with the following list of suggestions that will help you minimize stress, stay in balance, and create a successful college life.

1. Never give up. *Never giving up* is the mindset that you must maintain throughout your entire college stay. Giving up your college education can never be the solution to any seemingly unsolvable issue that raises its ugly head. Of course, there will be times when it will be easier to quit than to keep moving forward, but those are the exact times that you must not quit. It's like what my yoga teacher always says, "There will be days when you do not want to do your exercises but those are the *very* days that you must do them." Anybody can quit but it takes a special kind of person that can move forward in spite of obstacles. So, for any problems that try to knock you off your college path, I suggest you sit quietly, take long deep breaths, and figure out a solution that will keep you moving forward.

I once had a student in my writing class who was failing every paper. Since I allow my students to rewrite their papers for a passing grade, her course work grades averaged to seventy percent; but she was so frustrated by the fact that she had had to rewrite every paper that she did not believe she could pass the final exam essay. (You have to pass the final exam essay to get out of the course.) She did not show up to take the final. I found out from one of her classmates that she had become hopeless. I told her classmate to encourage her to return to class to take the retake-final exam. Since she did not show up for the final exam, that part was over, but she could still take the retake-final exam. (If students fail the final exam essay they get a second chance with a retake-final exam essay that, of course, has a new set of essay questions.) Well, this student did show up to take the retake-final exam and guess what? Yes, a happy ending; she passed. But what if she hadn't passed the retake-final exam? Would it have been the end of the world? Of course not. If you fail a course, just take it again and pass it with flying colors. Also, make sure you understand all the steps that you took that caused you to fail so that you can prevent failing another course. Use what you learn from a failure as a stepping stone to future success.

2. Focus on one class at a time. Please do not misunderstand me. I am not telling you to take only one class a semester or anything like that. I am saying that no matter how many classes you take, focus on handling one class at a time. Here's the deal. Every now and then you do have to look at the big picture—that's why you have your five-year plan. However, you should only put your energy into the work load of one class at a time. In other words, while you are in that class, be in that class. Stay fully focused on the lecture, discussion, group work, and other activities. Do all that is required in and out of that class. Set aside a specific regular time to study for that class. Do not sit in one class doing homework for another class. When you are in another class, stay focused in that class and set aside a specific regular time to study for that class. In other words, compartmentalize what is required for each class.

Let me explain further. I once took French and Spanish in the same semester. Of course, my family and friends thought I was crazy, and to be honest, I was a little concerned about whether I could handle two languages in the same semester myself; but I did not want to wait to take them in separate semesters. So I created a written plan on how to keep the languages separate. First, I made sure to take the classes on different days, say Spanish on Mondays and Wednesdays, and French on Tuesdays and Thursdays. Then I decided to attach my lab and study time for that particular class on the same days that the classes were held. In other words, I would go to Spanish lab on Mondays and Wednesdays; and I would go to French lab on Tuesdays and Thursdays. With regard to studying, I made sure to study and do my homework for the two languages on separate days or at the very least hours apart like Spanish in the morning and French in the evening.

The key, for me, was to get my brain used to the different times and days for each language so that I could be fully focused. I made every effort to stick to a very rigid schedule. This system actually worked very well with one tiny snag. Every now and then I would respond to an oral question in my Spanish class by answering in French or to an oral question in French class by answering in Spanish. It would always be when I did not know the answer in that language. Interestingly enough, I never answered in English. My brain would provide the answer in the other foreign language probably because it knew it needed a foreign language. I thought it was quite an interesting phenomenon although my professors were sometimes more than a little irritated. You would have thought I was responding in the wrong language on purpose.

3. Be efficient. Do not waste your valuable time doing things that have no real benefit for you. Yes, I am clear on what I just said so I suppose you are wondering what you could possibly be doing that is of no benefit. Let me give you a very clear example. Are you the gossipy type or have friends who like to gather and gossip? Do you really have time to waste gossiping with all that homework to complete? (I really don't understand how anybody has time to ever gossip anyway but that's another book.) What benefit is there for you in talking about someone else in the "he said, she said" vein when regardless of what he said or she said, you have a college life to manage. All gossip does is keep you from your tasks at hand whether it is college-related like studying or personal-related like taking care of your errands so that you can have more time to study. All gossip does is leaves a bad taste in your mouth and puts you in line to be the next person to be gossiped about.

There is also no benefit in socializing or partying or hanging-out or whatever to the point that you miss classes, homework assignments, or your daily responsibilities. Don't get me wrong. Socializing has its place but its place must be behind your responsibilities not in front of them. Socializing should enhance your life not take over your life. The bottom line is that you should make sure that your time is well-spent advancing your education as well as your life in a positive direction.

4. Stay balanced. Whenever you feel rushed or whenever you are having that feeling that there is not enough time to get everything done, sit down, have a cup of tea, and mentally walk through your day. I am sure that you will find places where you can use your time more efficiently. Get rid of those time busters and balance your studies, your work, and your personal life. The key word really is "balance." How does that phrase go? All work and no play make Jack a dull boy. Or all work and no play make Jill a dull girl. Well, all studying, work, and daily responsibilities can make college life pure drudgery. Yes, you must be efficient but efficiency includes allowing space in your life for enjoyable activities. In other words, do whatever it takes to get the most knowledge and the best grades from your classes but at the same time, do not let college life consume you such that college becomes your total life. (Of course, if "fun" for you is letting college be your total life, that's fine too.)

But for most people, college will be enjoyed better if sprinkled with regular fun and relaxation whether that includes taking long walks in the park, going to the movies, eating out at fabulous restaurants, or just reading great books. The key is to do what is fun and relaxing for you. Going to college should not stop your life! Going to college should be one positive aspect of your life.

5. Be responsible. Unfortunately, when students are told to be "responsible" they are offended as if one should assume that they are responsible simply because they are attending college. But responsibility goes beyond just signing up for courses. Being responsible is showing up for every class and showing up on time. Being responsible is making sure that you find out what you missed if you do miss class. Being responsible means showing up ready to learn with paper, pen, dictionary, homework, and all the necessary tools for learning. Being responsible means showing up with a clear mind that is ready and open to what the professor has to offer. In summary, being responsible means showing up well-rested, well-nourished, well-equipped, well-mannered, and well-disposed toward learning.

6. Have a contingency plan. If you have lived longer than a day, you know that things do happen when you least expect it no matter how well you plan. Although some of these things are *real* emergencies; that is, both unexpected and devastating, most emergencies are typical enough that you can have a contingency plan. Let me explain. Let's say you are a parent who has a babysitter taking care of your children while you are in class. What is your plan if the babysitter cancels an hour before you are supposed to leave for class? Will you have to miss your class? Absolutely not! You have a contingency plan. You have made sure that you have two or three people like family members, close friends, or trustworthy neighbors who you can depend on to watch your children at a moment's notice. You have even found a safe and responsible childcare center that allows parents to drop off their children for a few hours without advance notice.

How about some other scenarios? What about your car not starting just before you plan to drive to class? Do you have someone that can give you a ride to class and pick you up after class? What about car trouble on the way to class? Are you a member of an auto club or do you have car insurance that provides roadside assistance? And then, do you have someone who can come to your aid to take you onward to class? Imagine other scenarios that require contingency plans like your printer crashing in the middle of printing a research paper due the following day. (Of course, this could never happen to you because you printed your paper at least three days in advance, right?) Worse than that, what would you do if your computer crashed and you lost the research paper all together? Well, the smart organized student will have both a fairly recent backup copy on an external drive as well as a printed copy. The stressed, wait-until-the-last-minute student will have to find another computer, stay up all night and start all over again, or face the professor without a paper.

Having a contingency plan first requires that you prepare for what can go wrong by creating workable solutions for emergency scenarios. The goal is to keep your life moving forward. You want to protect yourself as much as possible from missing a class or turning in late assignments. (And know this. Some professors do not accept late assignments if they have given you weeks in advance to complete the assignment.)

7. Stay healthy. Have you heard the phrase, "An apple a day keeps the doctor away?" Well, I have also learned that an orange or two at the onset of a cold is the best safeguard against getting that cold. With regard to your college life, eating healthy will help to eliminate missed classes due to illness. Did you know that eating good foods and drinking plenty of water will increase your mental and physical energy? Did you know that walking, running or doing some other physical exercise for thirty minutes at least three times a week will minimize stress? Let one of your college goals be to create healthy eating, sleeping, drinking, and exercise habits. Do not forget meditation and yoga for increased calm and relaxation.

8. Compete with yourself. There is something about going to college that oftentimes makes a student feel competitive. There is nothing wrong with competing but do not put yourself in a stressed state by trying to keep up with other classmates. Instead compete with yourself. *Stretch yourself beyond old limits.* Always try to improve. If you made a "C" on your last test, then you should work toward making a minimum of "B" on the next test. Besides earning good grades, you should compete with yourself on how well you listen in class, how well you take notes, and how well you ask questions.

Also, compete with yourself by turning your weaknesses into strengths. On the first day of class, I always ask my students to list their strengths and weaknesses with regard to the subject matter. Interestingly enough, most of them are quite clear on their weaknesses. So I ask them how long their weaknesses have been weaknesses. They look at me dumbfounded. I say, "Well, once you knew you had a weakness, you should have started working toward turning your weakness into a strength. Weaknesses are not supposed to be weaknesses forever!" Do whatever it takes to turn your weaknesses around like seeing your professors during office hours, hiring tutors, and putting in extra study time.

9. Visualize success. Visualization is about creating mental images of how you want your college life to be. See only positive things. See yourself happily and peacefully participating and enjoying your classes. Imagine you are a huge sponge soaking up knowledge. See yourself learning without struggle. Visualize the grades that you desire. Make your visualization as detailed as possible and clearly picture your degree in your hand.

Take your visualizing to the material level with a visualization board that you can create by using a chalkboard, dry erase board, or whatever is handy for you. Post on your visualization board such items as inspirational pictures, symbols, words, and drawings from whatever media that suits your fancy. Write specific goals and be creative. Put whatever you want on your board that illustrates what you desire from your college life; that is, knowledge, good grades, the degree, the better job, and of course, peace and tranquility throughout it all. Place the board in a place where you can see it daily. Study it every day for several minutes to reinforce your visualization. Add, change, and rearrange items as you wish.

10. Celebrate your wins. All too often we rush through life without stopping to *smell the roses*. Some would say that we are just rushing to our deaths. With that in mind why not slow down, still get everything done, and enjoy your moments. As you accomplish certain milestones or get a hard-earned "A" on an assignment, take time to do something special for you. Even showing up to class after a hard day's work is worth treating yourself to your favorite candy bar. And what about patting yourself on the back after a long study period where your eyes hurt and your fingers ache. Doesn't such dedication deserve a reward? Of course, it does. Sometimes it is that little reward that gives you energy to work as hard on your next project. You must always take some time for you. It is your right. You are a college student now. You already deserve a celebratory cupcake!

Activity

Keep this book handy! Let it be your life support when you feel stressed. Feel yourself calm down as you re-read the segment that you need at that moment. Remember to breathe deeply and stay mentally positive to insure an enjoyable stress-free college life.

CPSIA information can be obtained at www.ICGtesting.com
Printed in the USA
LVOW081934240413

330728LV00002B/521/P